Mark Biddle

7th Dan W

The Heart of Taekwondo

Perfect Patterns   Achieve Power   Earn Promotion

7th Dan Kukkiwon

7th Dan Chung Do Kwan South Korea

7th Dan Chung Do Kwan Great Britain

Kukkiwon Instructor 2nd Class (awarded a letter of commendation for exemplary deed and outstanding conduct)

Photographs by Sean Neill

An Authors OnLine Book

Copyright © Mark Biddlecombe 2012

All rights reserved. No part of this publication may be reproduced, stored in a retrieval system, or transmitted in any form or by any means, electronic, mechanical, photocopy, recording or otherwise, without prior written permission of the copyright owner. Nor can it be circulated in any form of binding or cover other than that in which it is published and without similar condition including this condition being imposed on a subsequent purchaser.

British Library Cataloguing Publication Data.
A catalogue record for this book is available from the British Library

ISBN 978-0-7552-0705-3

Authors OnLine Ltd
19 The Cinques
Gamlingay, Sandy
Bedfordshire SG19 3NU
England

This book is also available in e-book format, details of which are available at www.authorsonline.co.uk

Dedication

I dedicate this book to my beautiful daughter. I love you.

Maisy Angela Valentine Biddlecombe

Contents

Dedication iii
Acknowledgements viii

1 The principles, structure and fighting spirit of Taekwondo 1
    Martial art
    The meaning of Taekwondo
    Tenets
    Status
    Belt system
    Developmental stages
    Change and movement
    Spirit
    Reflection

2 Black belt patterns 1-9: Philosophy 18
    Direction of travel

3 Physical and mental development 26
    Benefits
    Education
    Physical and mental power
    Exercise

    Feel-good factor
    Depression
    Obesity
    Self-esteem
    Self-confidence
    Appraisal

4 Taekwondo: A global cultural product   35
    World Taekwondo Headquarters
    World Taekwondo Federation
    Kukkiwon and WTF interrelations
    Reflection
    Globalisation
    Culture
    Identity
    Interrelations: Taekwondo and the world
    Taekwondo practitioners worldwide
    Taekwondo regional member nations
    Olympic sport
    Other martial arts membership

5 Standardisation of basic actions   54
    Stances, kicks, blocks and strikes

6 Kibon hand and leg drills   60
    Kibon hand drills 1-4
    Kibon leg drills 1-4

7 Fuel for the mind and body   69
    Dietary intake and physical performance
    Fuel for the mind and body
    Performance
    Recovery and repair
    An example of a healthy diet
    Harmonisation
    Reflection

8 Understanding patterns   85
    Patterns
    Aims
    Consciousness
    Performances: the self
    Applying oneself
    Competition
    Focused concentration
    Active meditation

9 Taegeuk patterns 1-8: Composition and philosophy   94
    Composition
    Taegeuk patterns philosophy
    The beginning of learning
    Kihap
    Actions
    Centre point of gravity
    Transition from Kup grade to Dan grade
    Basic kicking action

10 Power   111
    Developing power
    Strength and power

11 Breaking techniques   117
    Breaking techniques
    Material
    Speed and accuracy
    Expectations
    Distance
    Concentration
    Breathing
    Assistants
    Confidence
    Perfection

Conditioning
Breakable boards versus wooden boards
Breaking techniques on wooden and breakable boards: Procedure
Practising breaking techniques using breakable boards: Procedure

12 Dan grade promotion   129
    Grading
    Dan grade syllabus
    Expectations
    Promotion
    Discipline
    Attention to detail

13 Taegeuk patterns 1-8: Arrangement   139

14 Black belt patterns 1-9: Arrangement   199
    Reflection
    Final word

Appendices   280
Further reading   289

Acknowledgements

I would like to thank the following Grandmasters and Taekwondo Instructors for their friendship, trust and loyalty spanning more than 30 years. Their friendship and support has been inspirational and invaluable. This has helped me to attain personal goals which were beyond my imagination and expectation.

Grandmaster Park Hae Man, Grandmaster Karm Choy Vincent Cheong, Grandmaster Lindsay Lawrence, Grandmaster Graham Jones, Too Meng Ken, Jonathon David Barter, Brian Isaac Hussey, Patrick Donnelly, Colin Graves, Gerry Reilly, Vince Collins and Lynne Firth.

A special mention to Grandmaster Graham Jones; at over 70 years of age, he can still perform kicks at head height and with power. Through being continuously active, Grandmaster Graham Jones has remained agile, flexible and physically fit. He has always shown the greatest respect, dedication and commitment to the 'Taekwondo Chung Do Kwan'* family. Grandmaster Graham Jones is an inspiration to us all.

I would also like to thank Ann Frances Phillips for her continued encouragement and assistance with The Heart of Taekwondo. This has helped me to create a book with a unique style which will be an invaluable source of information in a Taekwondo practitioner's library.

*Chung Do Kwan literally means 'Blue Wave School'. The first school or Kwan to open in Korea was Chung Do Kwan, established in 1944. The 'Blue Wave' represents the 'Ocean Wave' and symbolises strength, power and determination. The ocean wave is relentless and never stops, characterised as a strong martial art fighting spirit. Grandmaster Park Hae Man, a world leader of the Chung Do Kwan family, at 80 years of age, still travels around the world conducting seminars. Grandmaster Park composed Ilyeo poomsae (9th Dan black belt pattern); he is truly a remarkable man. Grandmaster Lindsay Lawrence, president of Chung Do Kwan Great Britain, is a great example to us all. His name can be seen at the Kukkiwon Museum no less than 3 times, winner of 3 World Championship medals. Grandmaster Lindsay's martial art fighting spirit is exceptional, his style is unique, amazing. Today, Chung Do Kwan has global status and follows the complete curriculum of Kukkiwon (World Taekwondo Headquarters).

The Chung Do Kwan Great Britain website address is: www.chungdokwan.org.uk. You can also get in touch with Grandmaster Mark Biddlecombe via the Chung Do Kwan Great Britain website, or for direct contact: email biddleco@btinternet.com. This books website address is www.theheartoftaekwondo.com

Chapter 1

The principles, structure and fighting spirit of Taekwondo

Martial Art

Part of the success that has transformed a 2000-year-old fighting system into a modern sport lies within the structure and the ideals that underpin Taekwondo at local, national and global levels. Clubs, Associations and National bodies provide systematic structure and regulations that encourage Taekwondo practitioners to explore the martial art and progress through the ranks of a hierarchical grading system. The history and traditional values of past Taekwondo culture have not been forgotten. Principles such as etiquette, perseverance and spirit that guide behaviours remain deeply embedded within Taekwondo today. This book explores the structure and principles of the martial art. These are both separate entities and yet massively interwoven. Set forms or patterns, a continuous sequence of defensive and offensive techniques, are essentially at the heart of Taekwondo. New patterns are learnt at every stage of promotion and are rewarded with, and recognised by, the colour of the belt worn around the waist, usually white, yellow, green, blue, red and black. Promotion is not possible without acquiring the knowledge of a pattern and developing the ability to demonstrate it. A Taekwondo practitioner's aims include: perfecting patterns, achieving power within patterns, and earning promotion.

The Meaning of Taekwondo

Taekwondo is a Korean martial art system of self-defence that has grown in popularity on a global scale. Taekwondo, meaning "the art of kicking and punching", can be written as Tae Kwon Do. Tae means "to kick or strike with the foot", Kwon means "to punch or strike with the fist", and Do means "the way or art of". This system of self-defence comprises blocks, strikes, kicks and take-downs or sweeps. Taekwondo allows practitioners to develop skills individually, with a partner and within mixed or segregated gender groups. Practitioners regularly complete routines that include aerobic, anaerobic and stretching exercises, set forms, pre-arranged sparring, free sparring, self-defence against grabs and holds, and breaking techniques, generally using wooden boards and plastic breakable boards. The philosophy of Taekwondo shapes trainees on a personal level and also incorporates values that are shared within the discipline and are taken beyond the Taekwondo School into individuals' homes and spiritual lives. Taekwondo has become known for its spectacular kicking skills. These are learnt, demonstrated and developed by practitioners. Emphasis is placed on the idea that the leg's longer and larger muscle group offer a longer reach and more powerful strikes, compared with the arm. The unique kicking skills, combined with the development of Taekwondo as a competitive sport, have contributed to the popularity of Taekwondo. In particular, over the last forty years Taekwondo has seen rapid growth, with 200 National members spanning the globe. This led to its inclusion as a demonstration sport in the 1988 Olympic Games, Seoul,

South Korea. In the 2000 Sydney Games in Australia, Taekwondo gained recognition as an official event of the Olympic Games programme, becoming one of the most popular modern martial art sports in the world.

Tenets

Taekwondo practitioners aim to adhere to specific goals and attitudes, for example:

- To achieve the most accurate possible defensive and offensive techniques within a pattern.
- To develop the ability to execute techniques with speed and power.
- To achieve objectives and personal goals, such as promotion.

Training within the martial art incorporates physical and spiritual factors that are interwoven with the tenets of Taekwondo. The mind and body can be looked at as separate; the mind controls intellectual and emotional responses, which contrasts with the physical, material body. In a physiological sense, the mind is an emergent property of the brain. This implies that the body can not function without the mind and that the mind cannot exist in the absence of the body. The values that underpin Taekwondo suggest that training one's body and mind improves health and emotional stability, creating harmonisation of the mind and body. To achieve a healthy mind and body, training incorporates values such as discipline, perseverance and patience.

In practice, Taekwondo can be described as a discipline that draws on ideals that encourage certain behaviours and contribute to the practitioner's experience, joy and education of the art. The code of conduct, five principles or tenets that become part of the individual, are character-forming, namely: etiquette, modesty, perseverance, self-control, and indomitable spirit. Practitioners are encouraged to conduct themselves in a manner that adheres to this code. Attitudes and the understanding of the spirit of Taekwondo are learnt within the gymnasium and carried with the individual into other social circles. Physical training takes place inside the gymnasium and the spirit of Taekwondo is strengthened through social interactions. Thus, Taekwondo becomes a way of life.

Etiquette, rules of acceptable behaviour, is encouraged within and outside the gymnasium. Social expectations include traits such as respect, courtesy, to be polite, thoughtful and considerate. This creates a friendly, supportive and honest environment in the gymnasium.

Modesty relates to the way in which communication takes place; portraying good manners and being humble. Practitioners are encouraged to downplay their achievements, their skills and ability, to avoid boastful acts that may appear to be overbearing or arrogant. Practitioners of all grades are expected to mutually co-operate in order to further understand and refine their skills - promoting satisfaction, enhanced self-confidence and self-esteem.

Perseverance, linked with patience, is an essential element that enhances personal progress. The accomplishment of individual goals, fulfilling old and new challenges requires perseverance and patience. Obtaining a new grade, perfecting technical skills or breaking old habits, for example, can take weeks, months or years. The drive or self-belief to improve, to succeed, comes from within; it is about not giving up.

Self-control is one of the core tenets of Taekwondo. Training requires practitioners to practice disciplined routines on a frequent basis with an appreciation of the rules and values that form an integral part of the martial art. Demonstrating commitment by attending weekly lessons is in itself an act of discipline. Taking into consideration that training involves practising within social groups of mixed ability, the capacity to control the mind and body, the emotions and desires that influence behaviour, the control of an individual's actions and reactions, are crucial for the safety of the practitioner and others in the vicinity. In a sense, the ability to make decisions requires strength of mind; instructors and practitioners must ensure practical routines are kept within the capabilities of individuals, which ensures a safe, healthy and happy environment.

Indomitable spirit is concerned with courage and the desire to continue against overwhelming odds. To overcome obstacles or challenges, participants must continue to train hard, remain focused with a positive attitude and to never give up. This commitment and dedication, combined with an unassailable spirit, will mean different things to participants at different times, such as improvements of kicking and punching skills, flexibility and muscle strength. Objectives and personal goals can only be met over time, drawing upon attributes that are central to the concept of the practitioner's indomitable spirit.

The tenets are attributes that are achievable for all human beings. Taekwondo training encourages practitioners to be polite, humble, patient, considerate and courageous. Collectively, the tenets are looked upon as disciplines forming part of the spirit that surrounds the Taekwondo practitioner and shapes behaviour. Training on a regular basis, for instance one or two times a week, with an awareness of the values that underpin Taekwondo, helps to build character, promote friendship, loyalty, and confidence in everyday life.

Status

The relative position of the practitioner within Taekwondo is recognised by the colour of the belt worn around the waist.

Reputation and standing are accredited with an official title, such as Student or Instructor, which acknowledges and admires the level of attainment. Patterns increase in complexity and intricacy throughout the two-stage grading system and require the practitioner to mature in a similar way. Technical and mental skills develop in terms of, for example, speed, power, balance, flexibility, accuracy and focus. The difficulty of the patterns and expectations set within the framework of Taekwondo at Student level is considerably easier compared to the objectives at Master level.

Grade		Status
• Coloured belt holder	10th Kup – 1st Kup	Student
• Black belt holder	1st Dan – 5th Dan	Instructor
• Black belt holder	6th Dan – 7th Dan	Master
• Black belt holder	8th Dan – 10th Dan	Grandmaster

Belt System

One's progress or promotion through the grading system of Taekwondo is an illustration of the indomitable spirit, the strength of mind to progress, persevere and succeed. The belt system is structured, based on a hierarchical concept consisting of two main strata: coloured belts and black belts. The coloured belts are referred to as Kup grades, which means 'boy' or 'student'. In contrast, the black belts are referred to as Dan grades, which means 'man' or 'instructor'. The first stage of education within Taekwondo begins with the coloured belts. The lowest ranking coloured belt is white (10th Kup), and black tag on red belt (1st Kup) is the highest. The second stage is to work through the ranks of black belt. The lowest grade of black belt is 1st Dan; the highest grade of black belt is 10th Dan. The belt system is an indicator of how far a practitioner has progressed and the potential journey ahead. In the gymnasium, the practitioners stand in line according to their rank. The highest grade usually stands in the front of the class, with lower grades lined up behind. Each coloured belt, including the black belt, has its own philosophical meaning reflecting the knowledge, experience and growth that lead to maturity. This can be compared with other forms of life, such as plants or trees, and associated with the four classical elements that support life: earth, water, air and fire.

- White belt: White is pure, innocent, which reflects the beginner, who has no knowledge of Taekwondo. It is like an unplanted seed that has not started to grow.

- Yellow belt: Yellow represents the earth, which offers a solid base, a foundation that provides access to the basic knowledge and concepts of Taekwondo. The seed has been planted in the earth and has established roots. The plant has not broken the surface of the earth.

- Green belt: The beginner has advanced to an intermediate level, representing growth and strength. The young seedling has broken through the surface of the earth and matured into a fully grown tree, reaching up towards the sun, which provides warmth and direction.

- Blue belt: This advanced stage signifies maturity, standing in awe at the capacious boundaries of the sky, reflecting on seemingly unlimited learning possibilities that Taekwondo has to offer. The sky or heavens provides the water (rain) necessary to sustain life.

- Red belt: Red represents danger. Practitioners must exercise caution when making decisions during activities. Knowledge of advanced techniques, combined with the practitioner's development of strength and power, could cause injury to others, particularly during fighting routines. The ability to demonstrate self-control is essential as the first stage of learning comes to an end.

- Black belt: Black is the opposite of white; the status of the practitioner has grown or matured from a student to an instructor. The first stage has come full circle to completion; the Kup grade is now a Dan grade, which is associated with a high degree of proficiency and competence. The second stage, the transition from 1st Dan to 2nd Dan and above, has just begun; in this sense, black belt also means beginner. The practitioner must learn what it feels like to wear a black belt, to appreciate the status they have earned, to take on the responsibilities and uphold the tenets of Taekwondo. The real training can begin.

(a) Kup grade

Coloured Belt	
Rank	**Pattern**
10th Kup white belt	Basic techniques
9th Kup yellow tag on white belt	Basic techniques
8th Kup yellow belt	Pattern 1
7th Kup green tag on yellow belt	Pattern 2
6th Kup green belt	Pattern 3
5th Kup blue tag on green belt	Pattern 4
4th Kup blue belt	Pattern 5
3rd Kup red tag on blue belt	Pattern 6
2nd Kup red belt	Pattern 7
1st Kup black tag on red belt	Pattern 8

(b) Dan grade

Black Belt	
Rank	**Pattern**
1st Dan	Koryo
2nd Dan	Keumgang
3rd Dan	Taebaek
4th Dan	Pyongwon
5th Dan	Sipjin
6th Dan	Jitae
7th Dan	Chonkwon
8th Dan	Hansu
9th Dan	Ilyeo

Developmental Stages

The transition from one grade to the next grade, promotion from yellow belt to green tag on yellow belt, for example, requires practitioners to learn a new pattern. This process is repeated at practically every level throughout the coloured belt and black belt stages. In total, there are 20 grades and 17 patterns. Eight patterns are learnt within the 10 coloured belt stage and nine patterns are learnt within the 10 black belt stage. Each pattern varies, ranging from 18 to 30 steps, and progresses in difficulty in terms of both the number and complexity of defensive and offensive techniques. The process of learning a new pattern is progressive. It follows developmental stages; for instance, learning the initial sequence of movements, developing power and achieving a level of understanding that incorporates the spirit and philosophy attached to each pattern. Practitioners draw on the tenets of Taekwondo, helping them to advance through the two-stage grading system. Patience, perseverance and determination are crucial elements of the Taekwondo philosophy that equip the practitioner with the tools necessary in order to progress.

Initially, the sequence of movement within a pattern must be learnt in the correct order and practised repeatedly until the routine can be performed without conscious thought. Once the pattern can be demonstrated automatically, without thinking about the next move, hesitation is eliminated. This allows the pattern to flow easily from one step to the next. Speed and power will naturally improve within a free-flowing demonstration of sequenced actions. Practitioners must evaluate their own performance whilst demonstrating patterns, taking into account the effectiveness of the routine, calculating speed, power, balance, flexibility, and accuracy. The practitioner must shape the pattern to suit their own body structure and style with the aim of perfecting the pattern. The manner or attitude of the practitioner must include strength of mind, determination and focus in order to produce a routine that is strong in spirit, conviction and confidence.

In furthering their understanding of patterns, the practitioner must look at the philosophy and application or meaning of every defensive and offensive technique. Knowledge of the application of a technique provides the practitioner with a sense of purpose. Specific target areas of the body, for instance the face, chest or abdomen, can be protected with accurate blocking techniques. Offensive strikes or kicking techniques can be targeted accurately to the same areas of the opponent's body.

Although many of the basic movements within patterns are similar, the philosophy of Taekwondo shapes the structure of patterns at each grade. Techniques within a routine that flow freely and change direction easily may illustrate strength of character that incorporates relentlessness and adaptability, which is associated with the classical element of water. Patterns that contain fast combinations of hand techniques resemble the high-spirited, fast-flickering motion of fire. Special breathing techniques, large jumping actions and wide arm movements are a reminder of open air space. People's homes, the place where they live, the earth, are associated with the defensive nature of the patterns. It is a place that people attach importance to, protect and defend if necessary. In this sense, the characteristics of the patterns are determined by the blocks, strikes, kicks or stances that are unique to or absent from each routine.

The practitioner must study each pattern closely in terms of strengths and weaknesses. A pattern may favour hand techniques, foot techniques or contain an even distribution of hand and foot techniques. The execution of techniques can be fast or slow, hard or soft, and strong or weak. Routines may emphasise strong blocking actions which lack speed or contain fast actions that are weak; relying on the execution of a technique with speed to generate power rather than muscular strength. Overall, the Kup grade and the Dan grade patterns offer a balanced framework that take into account all aspects of the martial art, leading the practitioner towards maturity, physical fitness, mental power and emotional stability.

An appreciation of the speed of a pattern will help the practitioner to develop rhythm and timing, guided to an extent by the nature of the routine. One combination of techniques may flow more easily than another; for example, the action of moving in consecutive steps is easier in a tall, short walking stance as opposed to a low, long forward stance. Patterns that contain special breathing motions, where respiration is controlled by exhaling slowly, take approximately four to eight seconds to complete. This brings the flow of the pattern to a stop and increases the overall time required to complete the exercise. Routines containing simple techniques as opposed to advanced and complex combinations are easier and quicker to demonstrate.

Figure 1.1   Walking stance   Figure 1.2   Forward stance

Practitioners must develop the ability to demonstrate patterns with physical and mental stamina. Patterns must be performed with power and focus throughout the whole routine. The level of power and sharpness must be maintained from the initial movement until the final step. The ability to demonstrate patterns without a lapse in concentration is not an easy task and requires strength of mind and body. The practitioner must be strong enough to withstand fatigue and perform the pattern with focused attention, avoiding distraction.

Completion is only possible over time, once the practitioner can produce a well-balanced pattern demonstrating correct techniques with an understanding of the application of each movement. Patterns must be performed without conscious thought and with appropriate speed and power. The energy or the fighting spirit expressed by the practitioner demonstrating a pattern should be visible to the onlooker. The philosophy attached to each pattern should be reflected within the performance of the pattern. Strength of mind is required to perform a pattern that contains special breathing exercises; patterns that contain hard blocking techniques require physical strength. Persistence, patience and determination are key elements in developing to this level of attainment. The evidence of such attributes signifies that the practitioner has matured in the understanding of the way of Taekwondo.

Change and Movement

An important underlying law of Taekwondo is the concept of 'change and movement'. For improving fitness and health, the principle of positive social change and an active lifestyle are essential. Taekwondo ambassadors working in communities all over the world, with the goal of popularising Taekwondo, present the opportunity for social change. Traditional ways of life, everyday routines change and re-form to include Taekwondo education. The creation of social activities became easier with the development of communication technologies, from printed pamphlets and newspapers to internet websites and emails. These tools are all important factors which assist in the growth of Taekwondo, uniting individuals and social groups in general.

Frequent and regular physical exercise can contribute positively to physical fitness and health, strengthening muscles, assist with weight management and enhance the immune system. Physical exercise also improves mental health, assists in the prevention of depression and promotes or maintains self-esteem. This is the 'way' in Taekwondo; based on the principle of 'change and movement', the quality of life is enhanced.

Spirit

Taekwondo aims to develop the practitioner into a physically and mentally healthy human being. The processes and practices that shape the practitioner focus on physical actions and movements. To achieve one's own objectives, the execution of defensive and offensive technical skills is combined with the desire to succeed. The attitude or spirit that underpins the actions of the practitioner includes motivation, a sense of purpose to improve, with the will and determination to execute correct movements. The same values and principles are not limited to the Taekwondo gymnasium, but can be applied within the practitioner's home, place of work or other social circles as a way of enhancing the quality of life. The spirit also reflects the overall presentation of practitioners, relating to their appearance or dress code. Good personal hygiene and a clean, tidy uniform are encouraged within the gymnasium. Further explanation of the characteristics and attitude that are linked with the Taekwondo spirit, also described as a fighting spirit, is discussed within the philosophy of nine black belt patterns (chapter 2). These play a crucial role in the development of the practitioner's strength of mind.

Reflection

I began practising Taekwondo at the age of sixteen. After formal schooling that incorporated sports as part of the curriculum, plus extra sports sessions after school hours, I missed the thrill and challenge that I had experienced while engaging in sports events at school. I was taking a trip to the town centre using a local bus route when I saw a banner advertising Taekwondo lessons. I abandoned my trip to town, got off the bus and walked into the training hall to investigate further. Initially, I had no idea what Taekwondo was, other than a type of martial art. I found that there was only one Taekwondo club in the South of England at that time. I began to learn that the style consisted of straightforward practical fighting techniques and exercises which were taught systematically within a hierarchical grading system. I particularly found this style of martial art appealing, as it suited the need I had for both a physical challenge and a practical approach to self-defence.

I can still remember some of my early experiences within Taekwondo. During my 6th Kup green belt grading, my sister was taking photos of me when I was performing side kicks. I overheard spectators commenting, "She is taking a lot of photos of him", and someone else replied, "Yes, but he is good". I realised that I was technically very good, even at a very early stage of training, but I had no idea that I would achieve the rank of black belt, and certainly did not expect to become one of the highest-ranked Dan grades in the country. The challenge for me was always against myself, to perfect techniques and to take my next grading when my Instructor asked me to. I would never put myself forward, out of respect and courtesy to my Instructor. I believe the challenge for everyone in Taekwondo is a personal one. I always aim to achieve realistic goals; for instance, improve overall fitness, flexibility or promotion.

The opportunities to train, compete, and learn new techniques in gymnasiums all over the world is one of the reasons that inspired me to progress and continue practising Taekwondo. I have experienced the opportunity to engage with others in taking forward the 'way' of Taekwondo, how to live within the philosophies. I have personally been honoured and privileged to have visited and trained with practitioners in South Korea, Italy, Germany, France, Scotland, Spain, Taiwan, Thailand, Chinese Taipei, USA, Hong Kong and Singapore. Within the UK, I have trained with practitioners from Argentina, Ireland, Wales,

China, Indonesia, Malaysia and Nepal, to name but a few. I have always gone out of my way to meet fellow practitioners at airports, arranged transportation, hotels, lunches and training or competition events. When I was 23 years old, I made my first trip to Korea. The reception and support I received on arrival at the airport and throughout my trip had a huge, positive impact on my ability to train effectively. I have never forgotten this. This type of approach, courtesy, politeness and support is expected and extended to all grades within the Taekwondo family. The spirit, joy, responsibilities and expectations are based on traditional Korean ways of life. Senior grades take on more responsibility and support lower grades. Co-operation, friendship, loyalty and trust are experienced throughout a life-long learning process.

Training continues.

Chapter 2

Black belt patterns 1-9 Philosophy

Koryo

The first black belt pattern, Koryo, must demonstrate the principles of determination, persistence and patience, expressed as a strong martial art spirit. This strength of character associated with the Korean people has been inherited through the ages. In part, because of Korea's geographical position, surrounded by Japan, China and Russia, and with access to the Pacific Ocean, the country has been repeatedly invaded and counter-invaded. Throughout its history, the Korean people have demonstrated great resolve and spirit to resist aggressors in battle. In 108 BC, the city of P'yŏngyang (then the Kingdom of Choson) was overrun by China. From the 13th century onwards, the Mongolians repeatedly invaded Korea. In more recent times, the Japanese occupied Korea from 1910 to 1945. The Korean people have shown tremendous strength of character, demonstrating a will, a spirit to never be beaten, to protect its own culture and identity.

Keumgang

The second black belt pattern, Keumgang, meaning diamond, symbolises hardness. Slow, powerful defensive movements incorporate special breathing actions that help to develop strength from within. The diamond block and twin low section block should be executed with controlled, unconquerable, intrinsic power resembling the diamond, one of the hardest substances known to man. Practitioners must complete the pattern with force, spirit and determination. The crane stance is particularly difficult to demonstrate without losing balance. Controlled breathing techniques must be completed in one continuous breath.

Figure 2.1   Diamond block demonstrated in the crane stance

Taebaek

Black belt pattern number three, Taebaek, is the name of a mountain in Korea, meaning bright mountain. This pattern can be viewed as oppositional to the principles that Keumgang draws upon, moving away from slow, powerful actions with emphasis placed on agility and speed. Taebaek contains no special breathing techniques that would inhibit the flow of the pattern; in contrast, the routine flows continuously with light, fast movements of the hands and feet. The actions must be performed swiftly, effortlessly and with good balance. Speed is associated with the dazzling, awe-inspiring light at the summit of a sacred mountain.

Pyongwon

Pyongwon, the fourth black belt pattern, means plain, symbolising a vast outstretched land, a place where people live, and a home. This pattern should be demonstrated with a degree of confidence and composure, with the appearance of being relaxed and powerful and not unsettled or hurried. The pattern should incorporate the communication of comfortable, peaceful, happy and content feelings, associated with the emotions attached to being in one's own home. The contentment should reflect a familiarity that has grown as the practitioner has progressed in skill and maturity, consistent with the expertise expected at this master-level pattern. Slow actions and flexibility are very important aspects in this pattern.

Sipjin

Black belt pattern number five, Sipjin, represents the decimal system. The numbering system is infinite, adaptable and ceaseless in development. The pattern should be performed with an awareness of adaptation, endless change and progress. The beginning of the pattern contrasts the free-flowing movements associated with the form Taebaek. Special breathing actions interrupt the flow of the pattern no less than eight times. This draws on the idea of progress grinding to a halt, taking the time necessary for reflection and change, before forging ahead to overcome obstacles. Using reflective learning, development and change can lead to progress and the achievement of personal goals. Slow actions and moderation are key attributes of this pattern.

Jitae

The 6th black belt pattern, Jitae, is practised by the practitioner who holds the rank of 6th Dan black belt. The grade is regarded with prestige, acknowledging the dedication, loyalty, respect, and ability of the practitioner on achieving such a high level of attainment. 6th Dan certificates and above, issued by the Kukkiwon, the World Taekwondo Headquarters, are signed exclusively by the President of Kukkiwon.

Jitae represents the Earth and the struggle that human beings endure in order to survive. This pattern is a reminder of the constant battle not only to lead a healthy existence, but to improve the quality of life. Jitae encompasses the ideals of Sipjin and endless change, incorporating the principles that are embedded within Keumgang, Taebaek and Pyongwon, reflecting on strength, speed, power and the desire to lead a harmonious existence. The first part of the pattern, steps 1-10, places heavy emphasis on the development of inner strength. Special breathing actions are performed six times within this section of the pattern. The middle part of the pattern, steps 11-24, should be demonstrated with continuous focus on speed and agility. The final part of the pattern, steps 25-28, returns to a place of tranquillity, allowing the practitioner to relax. The last four techniques should be executed with smooth, controlled movements. Jitae pattern is a reminder of the ways in which power is developed and demonstrated. Special breathing techniques illustrate power or strength that comes from within; it is unmovable, solid, and unwavering. The techniques in the middle of the pattern rely on speed to generate power. If speed is lacking, the movement is weakened and acts like a pushing motion, which impedes effectiveness and damage. Power is also reflected in the way practitioners act within their environment, exhibiting a relaxed manner, being in control and not phased by situational factors.

Chonkwon

The seventh black belt pattern, Chonkwon, represents the Sky. The boundaries of the sky are far reaching, overwhelming and contain great knowledge and ideas. The techniques within the pattern comprise large arm actions, and a high jumping, spinning kick, reflecting the lively, imaginative and intense presence of the sky. The practitioner should aim to demonstrate the pattern with imagination, high-spirited and joyous actions that reflect the energy and seemingly unlimited boundaries of the sky that can only be looked upon in amazement.

Hansu

Black belt pattern number eight, Hansu, means water. Water is adaptable, cleansing, sustains life and encourages growth and development. The raindrop grows into a lake, cutting its own path and leaving its mark on the landscape. The lake is gentle in nature, large, intimidating and yet friendly and powerful.

The direction of travel in which the practitioner executes sequenced defensive and attacking actions can be related to the cardinal and intercardinal points of a compass, such as north, northeast, south and southwest. The sequenced movement's direction of travel within Hansu progresses along the cardinal and intercardinal lines. This is unique to this pattern. All the other coloured belt and black belt patterns' direction of travel use the cardinal diagram. This suggests that water has no fixed shape, is likely to change, illustrating flexibility and balance. The pattern should be practised with continuous fluid movements that are smooth and graceful, resulting in powerful, effective techniques that are executed with ease.

Ilyeo

The ninth black belt pattern, Ilyeo, means oneness. The discipline within this pattern reflects harmonisation of the body and mind. Practitioners should aim to demonstrate the routine with a sound body, directly observable, and sound mind, not directly observable. The physical and intrinsic qualities consist of determination, effort and hard work combined with focus, concentration and eye control. The pattern must be executed with confidence and composure, illustrating power and effectiveness. Harmonisation is possible by training over a long period of time, achieving promotions through the levels of coloured belt and black belt grading system, demonstrating controlled offensive and defensive techniques interwoven with the spirit and principles of Taekwondo.

Practitioners must demonstrate Ilyeo pattern for promotion from 8th Dan to 9th Dan black belt. To be eligible for the test, practitioners must be a minimum 53 years of age. In order to perform Ilyeo pattern to an acceptable standard at this stage of life, practitioners must remain active and maintain a healthy body weight. Ilyeo pattern incorporates a flying side kick which provides a means of assessing a practitioner's way of life. A practitioner that demonstrates commitment and exercises regularly is more likely to be able to perform this difficult jumping technique, succeed in a promotion test and maintain a healthy existence.

Taekwondo offers the practitioner ways of learning and understanding the principles of 'change and movement' that are integrated within the routines of the martial art. Everyday life consists of routines or activities that involve movement. The practitioner's actions and reactions may in themselves lead to a better understanding, experience and education of Taekwondo. In this sense, the philosophy of Taekwondo connects the techniques practised within the martial art and the activities of everyday life. The mind and body are used as a single unit, to maximise power and effectiveness, to overcome obstacles and to find solutions by continually changing and adapting. Through change and movement, the aim is to improve and enhance the quality of life. This is the 'way' or 'spirit'; the 'do' in Tae Kwon Do, which represents the overarching principles and values that guide the practitioner's approach, attitude and behaviour inside and outside the gymnasium. Taekwondo is a way of life. Taekwondo is for life.

Direction of Travel: Patterns

The continuous sequence of defensive and offensive technique within patterns can move forward, backward, diagonal and to the left side or right side of a fixed starting point. The movements travel along imaginary lines and frequently change direction. The direction of travel can be associated with the cardinal and intercardinal points of a compass. The practitioner starts the routine facing North, with South behind them, East is on their right side, and West is on their left side. The cardinal points are 90 degrees apart. The sequenced movements may travel North: 0 or 360 degrees; East: 90 degrees; South: 180 degrees; and West: 270 degrees. The intercardinal points mark the midway point between the cardinal points, which are also 90 degrees apart. They are Northeast: 45 degrees; Southeast: 135 degrees; Southwest: 225 degrees; and Northwest: 315 degrees.

Figure 2.2 Cardinal and intercardinal points of a compass

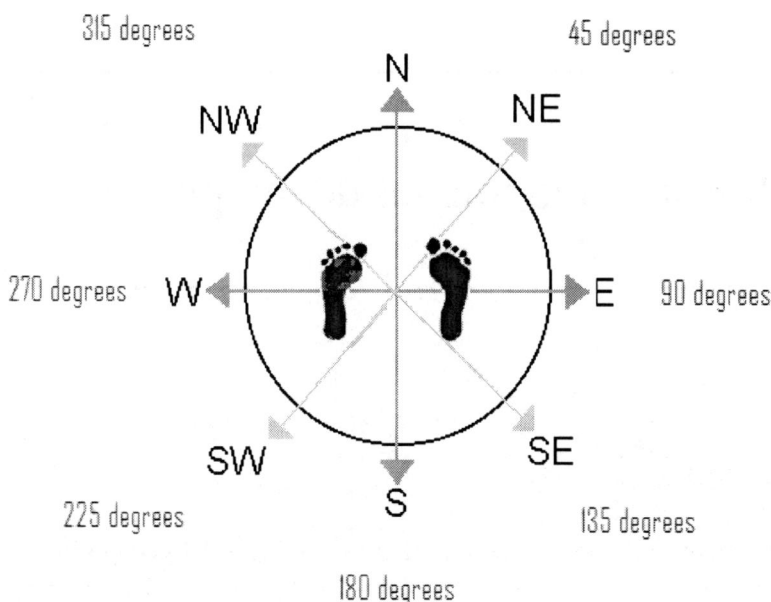

Training continues.

Chapter 3

Physical and mental development

Benefits

Physical and mental development is achieved by applying the philosophy and values of Taekwondo to the practical routines. Spirit - the attitude of determination to improve towards success without giving up - enables this process and encourages cultivation. Physical exercises, combined with a sense of achievement and rewards, promote a healthy body and mind and lead to harmonisation. Over time through participation, practitioners will strengthen physical power, develop mental power and discover the true nature of Taekwondo.

Figure 3.1   Harmonisation is achieved through a balance of physical and mental exercise

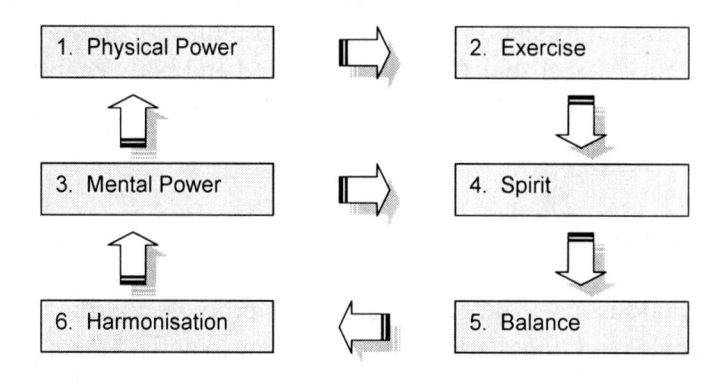

```
┌─────────────────┐         ┌─────────────────┐
│ 1. Physical Power│   ⇨    │  2. Exercise    │
└─────────────────┘         └─────────────────┘
         ⇧                           ⇩
┌─────────────────┐         ┌─────────────────┐
│ 3. Mental Power │   ⇨    │  4. Spirit      │
└─────────────────┘         └─────────────────┘
         ⇧                           ⇩
┌─────────────────┐         ┌─────────────────┐
│ 6. Harmonisation│   ⇦    │  5. Balance     │
└─────────────────┘         └─────────────────┘
```

1. Physical power is strengthened through physical exercises.
2. Physical exercises include, for example, defensive and offensive techniques, push-ups, sit-ups, running, skipping and vertical jumps.
3. Mental power is harnessed through motions and is linked with the approach, attitude and behaviour of the practitioner.
4. Mental power is strengthened through practising the patterns with an awareness of the spirit of Taekwondo and adhering to the disciplines that are embedded within the martial art. Practitioners, for example, must demonstrate focus, concentration, determination, eye control, breathing control and appropriate levels of speed and power.
5. Balance relates to the ability of a practitioner to correctly identify actions within a pattern that require mental processes and those that require physical strength. This should be demonstrated appropriately. Some patterns contain special breathing techniques that allow development of physical or mental strength and reveal the extent to which the practitioner has an understanding of these principles. These skills are developed throughout training and are finally mastered at 10th Dan, after thorough knowledge of all patterns has been

attained.
6. Harmonisation is achieved by practising all the patterns as a whole, as a single unit. Bringing the opposing sides, physical and mental aspects, together creates equilibrium and stability. A well-balanced, healthy mind and body enable the practitioner to feel good and enjoy a harmonious existence.

Education

Taekwondo is a self-defence system that promotes harmony and discourages fighting. Participants learn how to defend themselves by practising fighting skills which are encouraged only to be used as a last resort. An illustration of the nature of the martial art is reflected in the coloured belt and black belt patterns. The initial movement of every pattern places emphasis on a defensive blocking technique or action, which is usually followed by counter-attacking motions such as kicking, punching, thrusting or striking. Patterns are exercises that enable practitioners to learn and enjoy a self-defence system that began as part of Korea's culture. In Korea, Taekwondo is taught at schools to girls and boys from the age of five as part of the national curriculum and the police and the military are both highly trained in the discipline. Through education, the physical actions or movements and the spiritual, emotional aspects of the martial art are integrated.

Physical and Mental Power

The two-stage grading system incorporates clear objectives which involve learning and frequent practice of physical exercises and routines that gradually improve the practitioner's level of fitness and health. Having clear objectives provides a rationale for training and the motivation to train in a positive manner. Regular training encourages perseverance, as objectives are reached and new ones set. Through physical motion and repetition, the efficiency of routines improves and physical power increases. The body develops muscle strength, sustaining power, agility, flexibility, co-ordination, accuracy and balance. The way in which practitioners develop technical skills is integrated with spiritual aspects. Through physical activities, the mind improves in terms of concentration, focus, control and the ability to make judgements that may require self-restraint, whether training in a group or individually. Physical routines and mental awareness combined through training and repetition generates speed and power within the execution of defensive and offensive techniques. The practitioner should keep in mind the tenets and values of Taekwondo during activities and decision-making - acting in an appropriate, considerate, safe and helpful manner.

Exercise

The Taekwondo gymnasium offers the practitioner a home where physical exercises can be performed on a regular basis. Depending on the club or organisation, training usually takes place once or twice a week. Exercise leaves the body feeling warm, with an increase in the breathing rate and heart rate. There is overwhelming evidence that regular practical exercise enhances or maintains physical fitness, mental health and the immune system. People who lead an active lifestyle are more likely to feel happier and more satisfied, with an improved general sense of wellbeing. Fit people live longer.

Feel-Good Factor

During physical exercise, chemicals known as endorphins are released in the brain. These are known to have strong effects on mood, raising the pain threshold, enhancing euphoria and reducing emotions of anxiety and stress. Studies using PET scans (positron emission tomography) have revealed that higher levels of endorphins are produced during exercise compared to when the participant was not performing tasks. PET scans display images of neural brain activity on a screen in a similar fashion to x-rays. It was found that endorphins produced during exercise were attaching themselves to areas of the brain associated with emotions, mainly the limbic system and prefrontal cortex. This suggests that exercise contributes to a feeling of wellbeing and is potentially a preventative or method of treatment for disorders such as depression.

Depression

People suffering from mild forms of depression are often recommended thirty minutes a day of moderate exercise. This can have a very positive impact on their mental health. Depression is both a physical and mental illness incorporating a chemical imbalance in the brain. Thoughts, feelings and chemical brain activity are not separate items, but part of the same highly complex phenomenon. Feelings of sadness, lack of motivation, sleeping poorly, a sense of worthlessness and weight loss or gain, over an extended period of time, can indicate that a person is depressed. Situational factors such as redundancy or bereavement can be implicated in becoming depressed. However, this type of depression is essentially a reversible state. Psychological treatment may aim to change a person's behavioural routine and patterns of thought. There is strong evidence that taking part in weekly physical exercise has a positive impact on an individual's mental health state. Professionals often recommend that people suffering from depression engage in regular physical exercise. Psychological and drug therapies are complemented by exploiting the benefits of physical exercise. Chemical imbalances in the brain are implicated in depressive states. Depression can be helped with the use of antidepressant drug therapy. However, regular exercise can naturally raise the levels of endorphins in the brain; this leads to improvements in mood, increased self-esteem and weight management.

Obesity

For many people, an active lifestyle is essential for maintaining a healthy weight. Taekwondo offers a variety of physical exercises that help to deal with obesity and weight control. The energy used during exercise and the metabolic rate (chemical chain of processes inside the body that sustains life) uses up calories which are produced from the intake of food. The consumption of too much food and too little exercise results in excess levels of calories, which are not used and subsequently stored as fat. Achieving a balance between exercise and a healthy diet improves physical fitness. At the same time, mental health states improve, enhancing a general sense of wellbeing, confidence and self-esteem.

Figure 3.2 Weight management is achieved through a balance of energy intake and energy output

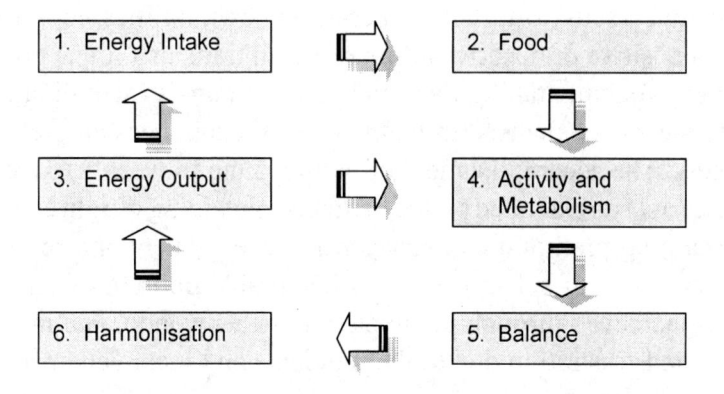

1. Energy Intake → 2. Food
↑ ↓
3. Energy Output → 4. Activity and Metabolism
↑ ↓
6. Harmonisation ← 5. Balance

1. Energy intake refers to the amount of calories consumed.
2. Food refers to dietary intake that is converted into calories and provides a source of energy.
3. Energy output refers to the amount of calories used.
4. Activity and metabolism relates to exercise and the rate that calories are processed.
5. Balance relates to the amount of food intake interwoven with the quality and extent of physical exercise.
6. Harmonisation is achieved by obtaining a balanced relationship between energy intake and energy output, without a surplus supply of calories. The aim is to lead an active, healthy lifestyle, fuelled by an appropriate amount of calories.

Self-Esteem

An individual's physique, combined with their self-image, has a direct impact on their self-esteem. Negative self-perceptions often contribute to depression. Exercise helps to shape the physical appearance of the body and also affects the mind. Regular, often predictable repetitive training improves psychological characteristics such as self-esteem, self-confidence and mental alertness. Self-esteem is an enduring personality characteristic which suggests how an individual evaluates or appraises their own worth, their good points, qualities, and moral values. An individual's self-worth, confidence in their own abilities, combined with a positive or negative attitude, are all traits that impact upon decision-making, taking risks and acting on one's own initiative. Self-esteem is enhanced through personal challenges and related success. The accomplishment of participating in weekly exercise classes over an extended period of time, maintaining weight control and earning promotion, deserves acknowledgement and respect. Higher levels of self-esteem or a favourable opinion of oneself can be achieved through participation in Taekwondo. Feelings of stress and frustration due to the problems and inconveniences of day-to-day life are less impacting on those who exercise regularly; they have more energy to deal with problems and are mentally and physically stronger than those who do not exercise.

Self-Confidence

Completing physical exercises or practical daily routines requires physical and mental energy. The effort that individuals exert may lead to improvement, success or sometimes result in disappointment or failure. Taekwondo practitioners are encouraged not to give up, but to remain determined, patient and persevere. The attitude needed to continue can be described as an act of confidence, a level of self-belief that enables individuals to take control, use their own initiative and make decisions in the pursuit of personal goals. Individuals who lack confidence may be described as timid, nervous, hesitant and afraid of failure. Self-confidence develops over time through repetitive acts. Frequent physical exercise or the interaction with practical daily routines builds confidence. Situational factors become familiar or well-known, which enable individuals to feel relaxed and comfortable. Self-belief or self-assurance increases the possibilities to overcome difficulties and accomplish objectives and personal goals.

Appraisal

Self-confidence and self-esteem are unlikely to develop if the risks and challenges, inside and outside the Taekwondo gymnasium, are beyond the capabilities of individuals. Appraisals of objectives and life events require realistic aims that are appropriate for the situation. Realistic expectations increase the prospect of achieving success. Taekwondo practitioners are encouraged to demonstrate courage, a fighting spirit, and adapt to the challenges that the martial art has to offer. Promotion through the coloured belt and black belt ranks requires practitioners to approach tasks with a positive attitude. Negative thoughts may lead to failure before the exercise has even commenced. Practitioners must be proactive and not wait for things to happen; build on their success and work on their weaknesses. They will be supported towards this by experienced instructors. The tenets of Taekwondo, interwoven with the principles of repetition, commitment and effort, are crucial factors that lead to the perfection of defensive and offensive techniques, and, ultimately, success.

In the process of Taekwondo education, practitioners discover their strengths and weaknesses. Physical and mental power, linked with a positive attitude and hard work, is enhanced through exercise. Physical, psychological and biological states change, adapt and mature. The practitioner's journey is not only rewarded with a healthy mind and body, but also praise and admiration on achieving promotion. In pursuit of perfecting patterns, the true nature of Taekwondo is discovered – although perfection is never really achieved.

Training continues.

Chapter 4

Taekwondo: A global cultural product

World Taekwondo Headquarters

Taekwondo began as part of Korea's culture. Since the establishment of Kukkiwon (World Taekwondo Headquarters) in 1972, the martial art has seen rapid growth. Kukkiwon has provided organisation and structure to the presentation of the martial art across the world. This has helped to spread knowledge of Taekwondo at national and global levels. These structures and how they have been implemented have impacted positively on the general awareness of Taekwondo as a sport and discipline. This has resulted in increased global membership. Kukkiwon is responsible for the organisation and development of the traditional martial art.

World Taekwondo Federation

The World Taekwondo Federation (WTF) was established in 1973 to manage and develop competitive sports events. The martial art and competitive sport components can be described as disciplines that have divided or changed the direction of Taekwondo practice, its development and its future. Instructors and practitioners may select to study the traditional martial art system of self-defence and the modern-day fighting aspect of competitive sport. Kukkiwon and the WTF mainly focus on the regulation and development of their particular field. Both organisational bodies co-operate and work towards a common goal of promoting Taekwondo. The first secretariat of the WTF, in 1973, was placed and began operations at the Kukkiwon Headquarters.

Kukkiwon and WTF Interrelations

Figure 4.1   Taekwondo organisation and responsibilities

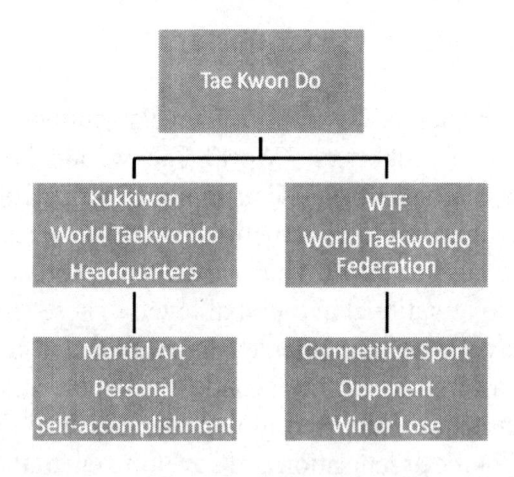

```
                    Tae Kwon Do
                   ┌─────┴─────┐
              Kukkiwon         WTF
          World Taekwondo  World Taekwondo
            Headquarters      Federation
                 │                │
            Martial Art    Competitive Sport
             Personal         Opponent
        Self-accomplishment   Win or Lose
```

Kukkiwon headquarters aims to support and develop the self within the martial art of Taekwondo. As members of the association, practitioners are expected to adhere to codes of conduct set by the association. Group membership is experienced alongside the pursuit of personal goals, such as promotion and status. Individual achievements are recognised and rewarded by Kukkiwon Headquarters with certification and a ranked grading system of coloured belt and black belt grades. Personal development and attainment is centred on practitioners being in competition with their selves. The WTF main criteria are focused on competitions. The results of competitive matches and the safety of the players are of the utmost importance. Practitioners are in competition with their opponent. The ultimate goal is to win.

Kukkiwon headquarters provide Dan grade certificates to practitioners that successfully pass promotion tests. These are usually issued through WTF-recognised national governing bodies. The procedures and technical standards required for all the levels of testing are regulated by Kukkiwon Headquarters. This includes the awarding of coloured belts and black belts. The WTF supports the decisions and actions of Kukkiwon in all matters concerning the procedures and criteria regarding Dan grade promotion tests. World Taekwondo Championships organised by the WTF specify that all participants are holders of Kukkiwon Dan grade certificates. In turn, the Kukkiwon organisation supports the WTF by making financial donations from revenue generated by Dan grade certification.

Promotion tests are not compulsory, although practitioners are encouraged and helped by instructors to test at appropriate and permitted times. Usually, a minimum training period of 3 months must have elapsed between each coloured belt grade before practitioners can test for promotion. Obligatory time periods for promotion extend through the black belt grading system. The minimum time required for promotion from 1st Dan to 2nd Dan is 1 year, from 2nd Dan to 3rd Dan is 2 years and from 3rd Dan to 4th Dan is 4 years. Application for Senior Dan grade examinations are also subject to minimum time requirements. Age limits also apply to the Dan grading. For example, practitioners testing for 4th Dan must be 21 years of age or over and for 4th Dan to 5th Dan the minimum age requirement is 25 years of age or over. Further interaction between the Kukkiwon and the WTF concern the winner of world level championships sponsored by the WTF. The gold medallist is entitled to privileges set by the Kukkiwon Headquarters, with minimum time and age limits required for promotion being reduced by 80 per cent. Probably the greatest accolade in sporting events is the winner of the Olympic Games. Taekwondo athletes who win the top prize are rewarded with reduced minimum training and age limits by 100 per cent, at the discretion of Kukkiwon Headquarters.

Publicity that has surrounded the Olympic Games and World Championships has promoted Taekwondo both as a sport and a martial art discipline. The immense power of media coverage has impacted on public perceptions of the martial art. It has allowed the values and spirit of Taekwondo to be spread throughout the world. Coverage of live sporting events on television often incorporates information about high-profile athletes. Fans are informed of not only the athlete's performance in the sporting arena, but also details of their characters and personal lives. Satellite television, the internet and mobile phones enable communication from one side of the globe to the other. This allows individuals to send information directly from sporting arenas to anyone who possesses the appropriate technology, throughout the world. The profile of sporting events is increased by these processes and has led to further interest in sports and growth in the participation of sports in general.

Kukkiwon Headquarters dispatches black belt Master grades to developing countries as ambassadors to teach Taekwondo so that people around the world can enjoy this traditional martial art system of self-defence and a world sport. Local clubs are encouraged to support such events and local advertising is often used to promote awareness within communities. This approach also provides revenue for Taekwondo and so optimism for the continuation of Taekwondo globally. World-wide public relations are strengthened through regular contact and continued support for all Taekwondo clubs around the globe. Eastern philosophy considers all Taekwondo clubs as belonging to the same family, promoting friendship, mutual respect and loyalty. Kukkiwon objectives include research and development of teaching methods, promotion tests and academic activities. The Kukkiwon Academy focuses on these aspects. Black belt courses are organised at

Kukkiwon Headquarters for domestic and oversees instructors; this includes standardisation of techniques, patterns, procedures and regulations of promotion tests. These aspects act to strengthen world-wide public relations. Global expansion ensures the short-term and long-term future of Taekwondo.

Changes to the infrastructure within Taekwondo (establishment of the Kukkiwon and the WTF) have had an impact on a global scale. Taekwondo leaders have transformed the martial art into a truly global cultural product, using innovative ideas that retain the over-arching values, principles and spirit of Taekwondo practice. Remarkably, since the establishment of the Kukkiwon Headquarters, Taekwondo gained recognition as a mandatory Olympic Games sport in only 30 years.

- 1972   The Kukkiwon World Taekwondo Headquarters, based in South Korea, was established. Since this time, instructor courses and seminars have been conducted on a regular basis. These include coaching, judging and refereeing for competitions and promotion tests. These courses are open to Korean people and 'foreigners'. There are courses open only to Korean people. Korean 3rd class, 2nd class and 1st class instructor courses, 1st class being the most advanced, are held usually once a year at the Kukkiwon.
- 1973   The WTF was established, initially based inside the Kukkiwon building, South Korea.
- 1973   The 1st World Taekwondo Championship was held at the Kukkiwon Headquarters.
- 1979   The WTF became an International Federation recognised by the Summer International Olympic Committee.
- 1988   Taekwondo was accepted as a demonstration sport at the Seoul Olympic Games, South Korea, for the first time in history.
- 1991   The Kukkiwon museum, memorial hall was founded. Artefacts include championship trophies, medals, certificates, badges and details of placing of competitors at major Taekwondo competitions, such as the World

Championships and the Olympic Games.
- 1992   Taekwondo was once again accepted as a demonstration sport at the Barcelona Olympic Games, Spain.
- 1998   3rd class, 2nd class and 1st class foreigners' instructors' course first established at the Kukkiwon.

Taekwondo: Significant achievement: Year 2000

- 2000   Taekwondo history was made when it was nominated as a mandatory sport at the Sydney Olympic Games, Australia.
- 2004   Participation in the Athens Olympic Games, Greece.
- 2008   Participation in the Beijing Olympic Games, China.
- 2008   Kukkiwon Headquarters established the 1st instructors' course for the differently abled.
- 2009   Kukkiwon Headquarters held the 1st Seoul World Leaders Forum with Master grade practitioners participating from all over the globe.
- 2009   Ceremony of Taekwondo Day, commencement of the construction of 'The Taekwondo Park'.
- 2012   Participation in the London Olympic Games, England.

Taekwondo: Huge investment for the future: Year 2013

- 2013   Completion of Taekwondo Park, which started construction in 2009. This unique 570 acres site is nestled into landscape surrounding Baekun Mountain, Muju, South Korea. The facility is designed to become a world cultural heritage centre, promoting Korean culture and art, catering for tourists, Taekwondo practitioners, Taekwondo professionals and Taekwondo federation administrators. The project has investment of over 500 hundred million US Dollars. Three core areas of the park are named The Spirit, The Mind and The Body. The Body contains a competition arena with the capacity to hold 5000 spectators. The Mind holds traditional Korean-style buildings and training areas for the development and research of Taekwondo techniques and education. The Spirit is an area of open space and beauty that symbolises harmonisation: a place where Grand Masters can reflect in nature-friendly settings. Ascending pathways, waterways and bridges link the body, mind and spirit which represent the Taekwondo practitioner's journey, the novice white belt aspiring to the level of Grand Master black belt. The location, design and innovation have produced a stunning, spectacular Taekwondo Park within a mountainous landscape that combines nature and culture peacefully.

- 2016   Confirmation for participation in the 2016 Olympic Games as an official sport. Approved by the International Olympic Committee (IOC). (Information disseminated in 2009.)

Reflection

I have been very fortunate to have personally witnessed, and been a part of the process that has transformed Korea's home-grown martial art system of self-defence into a globally recognised cultural product. In 1988, I was in South Korea watching Taekwondo practitioners competing for medals in the summer Olympic Games. This was a remarkable exhibition of skill and courage which marked a major turning point in the history of Taekwondo. Up until this time, a relatively unknown sport was being televised and talked about across the globe.

In 2001, I was a participant in the 4th Foreigners' Taekwondo

Instructor Training Course, 3rd Class. Only a handful of Instructors in the UK had successfully completed this course. In 2006, I completed the 12th Foreigners' Taekwondo Instructor Training Course, 2nd Class, and was awarded a letter of commendation for exemplary deed and outstanding conduct. I would recommend that all Instructors visit Korea and take part in the Instructor courses. My experience of training at the Kukkiwon, the World Taekwondo Headquarters, is of hard work; it is exhilarating and great fun. It provided a crucial enhancement to my confidence. It reaffirmed that methods and techniques that I had been teaching were in line with Kukkiwon standards.

In 2009, I attended two events that were unprecedented historical events. Approximately 200 VIP Kukkiwon Masters, from over 50 countries, were invited to share their ideas and experience at the '1st Seoul World Taekwondo Leaders Forum'. I felt honoured and privileged to receive a personal invitation to the event. I have kept the letter as a prized possession. The occasion was very formal. It brought me in to an area of Taekwondo that I had not experienced before. I had been invited to give input through focus groups, working dinners, cocktail parties and social engagement. This felt like I was now engaging in the business side of Taekwondo, in Korea, and representing the practitioners within the UK. The hospitality I experienced was parallel to hospitality extended to top executives within international businesses. Throughout all proceedings, I was impressed with the spirit, friendship and etiquette that framed all interactions and were extended to all. I had now entered the higher levels of the business side of Taekwondo and found that even at the highest levels, the philosophies are practised.

In the same month of 2009, I was at the 'Ceremony of Taekwondo Day, commencement of the construction of The Taekwondo Park'. This was the first brick-laying ceremony of a huge development that would assist in ensuring the long-term future of Taekwondo as a global martial art and Olympic sport. We were standing within a beautiful mountainous landscape, on a very hot sunny day with clear blue sky. I could not help but look around in awe at the majestic surroundings. I completely forgot that I was wearing a tailor-made suit with shirt and tie. The occasion was amazing, with formal speeches, dancing and singing, Taekwondo demonstrations and fireworks. The Taekwondo Park will be a huge success and attraction for Taekwondo practitioners and tourists, and I was there, right at the beginning; what a privilege!

Globalisation

Education, knowledge and a commitment to life-long learning are probably the greatest tools that lead to innovation, competitiveness and positive change. Education and new knowledge provides opportunities and choices that may not have materialised within isolated or fixed communities where cultural practices have remained practically unchanged for centuries. In the Western World the transmission of vast amounts of knowledge is virtually instantaneous. Modern communication technologies such as satellite television, the internet and mobile telephones connect different countries and communities across time zones and vast geographical expanses. Globalisation can be described as a process that ignores territorial boundaries of nation-states. Organised Transnational networks cut across borders virtually free from the control of authority and governmental bodies. Geographical distance disappears with the use of bulletin boards, websites and e-mail, bringing together different parts of the world and facilitating new relationships.

Taekwondo leaders have developed the martial art to include the Kukkiwon headquarters and the WTF. Both of these work separately and in conjunction within the Taekwondo framework, which provides structure, finance, stability and support on a greater scale. This helps Taekwondo to expand and grow within a competitive world market. Western products that have global status include, for example, Disney, Coca-Cola and McDonald's.

Logos associated with these companies have become easily recognised across the world. The yin and yang symbol has also gained recognition in association with the martial arts in a similar fashion. It is an indication of how pervasive and subtle advertising can be in affecting cultural perceptions. The 'shrinking' of the world by process of globalisation has allowed the erosion of some ridged cultural practices and transformed the shape of communities. This can be viewed as a positive element, where tolerance and understanding of other cultures exist. Multicultural societies provide opportunities never imagined 50 years ago. Organisations that possess the infrastructure, access to modern communication networks, have greater potential to expand and grow in what seems to be a smaller world.

Taekwondo is both a life style, and a product that has influence globally. Developing countries may not have adequate systems in place, with regions that are geographically isolated or circumstances of inequality prevent access to appropriate systems of communication. In addressing these issues, Kukkiwon Headquarters dispatch Master grade instructors to support other countries. Through this process, the dispersal of Taekwondo education is able to reach new territories. Both the Kukkiwon and supported country benefit from potential expansion and growth. Sensitive approaches in presenting new ideas and different ways of thinking are crucial in the development of working relationships. Kukkiwon ambassadors are encouraged to act in ways that reveal their respect for individual cultures and that show incite in to ways of enriching the quality of life through Taekwondo philosophies. This approach allows principles of change and movement within specific communities to be realised.

Figure 4.2   Planet earth, a borderless world

This illustration of planet Earth in space shows no roads or borders. Boundaries, communities and nations are not apparent. It serves as a reminder of how small the world has become through the phenomenon of Globalisation.

Culture

Globalisation has made the possibility of travelling and migration easier. The explosion of knowledge-sharing, the ease of making travel arrangements and economic interchange has been made possible at almost unimaginable speed. Once isolated or remote societies can now be interconnected. Over an extended period of time this may cause fragmentation and re-forming of cultures. New cultural norms may emerge and combine with traditional ways of life. Taekwondo offers the opportunity to create multicultural practices that bring people closer together. Principles of change and movement (See chapter 1) are integrated within the routines of the martial art and practised by all members of the organisation. The shared codes and practises do not recognise cultural or racial division. Taekwondo practitioners experience the opportunity to train together, regardless of background, for the promotion of friendship, trust, joy and excitement in the society where they live and alongside fellow members of the Taekwondo family.

Identity

Taekwondo links the personal to the social. Individual identities and social identities provide people with a sense of who they are. People who have a common interest, such as martial art practitioners, share a collective identity. Group identities are not confined to local communities, but incorporate national and global bodies that have shared interests. Individual identities may include being a mother, father, son, daughter or someone who enjoys listening to music. Individual identities are part of everyday life and include interactions with people that are perceived as the same or different from us. Different roles are adopted by individuals according external expectation and personally held perceptions. A female may act as a mother before the school day begins and a worker during the day. She may become a member of a local Taekwondo club and then take on the role of a Taekwondo practitioner in the evening. This suggests that identities are fixed and fluid, changing and re-forming. Identities involve how people see themselves and how others see them, an awareness or consciousness of who they are, who they can become and the associated roles.

Knowledge is strengthened by the process of life-long learning. Globalisation encourages the spread of knowledge-based systems which could lead to the formation of multicultural societies.

According to the principles of change and movement, taking part in weekly exercise classes involves being active, taking on roles and acting them out. Individual differences are minimised when practitioners take on a group identity. In this sense collective identities create a cohesive society.

Taekwondo Masters travel the world with the aim of providing communities with the opportunity to practice and learn a martial art that began as part of Korea's culture. Physical regular repetitive exercise enhances the performance of the mind and body. Self-confidence, self-esteem, feeling physically and mentally stronger are all achieved through an active lifestyle. Taking the first step into a gymnasium is probably the hardest part. Behaviour and attitudes change to incorporate training sessions as part of everyday life. In the process, new identities and cultural practices are formed. The disciplines, values and principles embedded within Taekwondo philosophy help to enhance and generate a new way of life.

Interrelations: Taekwondo and the World

Taekwondo within its modern framework has captured the interest of and influenced millions of people. Membership levels are continually rising in all corners of the world. The innovation, support and marketing strategies of Taekwondo leaders have transformed the Korean martial art into a global cultural product and a world sport.

Taekwondo practitioners worldwide

The number of member nations that have joined the WTF is 200. Since the WTF was established in 1973 with a membership of 7 member nations, the association has continued to grow. Within the first 20 years, WTF member nations increased by nearly 100. Over the next ten years a further 50 nations had joined the association, making a total of 153 members. From the year 2000 to 2009, memberships had risen to 189. By 2012, memberships had risen to 200 member nations.

Figure 4.3   WTF Global Membership

Number of
Nation Members

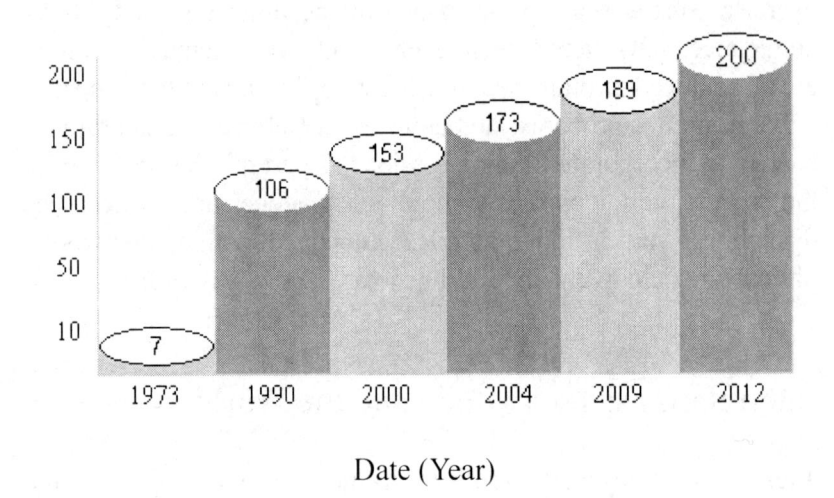

[Bar chart showing: 1973: 7, 1990: 106, 2000: 153, 2004: 173, 2009: 189, 2012: 200]

Date (Year)

Taekwondo regional member nations

Europe – member nations 49:

Albania, Andorra, Armenia, Austria, Azerbaijan, Belarus, Belgium, Bosnia and Herzegovina, Bulgaria, Croatia, Cyprus, Czech Republic, Denmark, Estonia, Finland, France, Georgia, Germany, Great Britain, Greece, Hungary, Iceland, Ireland, Isle of Man, Israel, Italy, Latvia, Lithuania, Luxembourg, Macedonia, Malta, Monaco, Montenegro, The Netherlands, Norway, Poland, Portugal, Romania, Russia, San Marino, Serbia, Slovak Republic, Slovenia, Spain, Sweden, Switzerland, Turkey, and the Ukraine.

Asia – member nations 43:

Afghanistan, Bahrain, Bangladesh, Bhutan, Brunei, Cambodia, China, Chinese Taipei, Hong Kong, India, Indonesia, Iran, Iraq, Japan, Jordan, Kazakhstan, Korea, Kuwait, Kyrgyzstan, Laos, Lebanon, Macao, Malaysia, Mongolia, Myanmar, Nepal, Oman, Pakistan, Palestine, Philippines, Qatar, Saudi Arabia, Singapore, Sri Lanka, Syria, Tajikistan, Thailand, Turkmenistan, United Arab Emirates, Uzbekistan, Vietnam, Yemen, and Timor-Leste.

Africa – member nations 45:

Algeria, Angola, Benin, Burkina Faso, Burundi, Cameroon, Cape Verde, Central African Republic, Comoros, Cote d'Ivoire, Congo, DR of the Congo, Egypt, Equatorial Guinea, Ethiopia, Gabon, Gambia, Ghana, Guinea, Kenya, Lesotho, Liberia, Libya, Madagascar, Malawi, Mali, Mauritius, Morocco, Mozambique, Niger, Nigeria, Rwanda, Sao Tome & Principe, Senegal, Somalia, South Africa, Sudan, Swaziland, Chad, Tanzania, Togo, Tunisia, Uganda, Zambia, and Zimbabwe.

Pan America – member nations 44:

Antigua & Barbuda, Argentina, Aruba, Bahamas, Barbados, Belize, Bermuda, Bolivia, Brazil, British Virgin Islands, Canada, Cayman Islands, Chile, Colombia, Costa Rica, Dominican Republic, Cuba, Dominica, Ecuador, El Salvador, Grenada, Guadeloupe, Guatemala, Guyana, Haiti, Honduras, Jamaica, Martinique, Mexico, Netherlands Antilles, Nicaragua, Panama, Paraguay, Peru, Puerto Rico, St. Lucia, St. Kitts & Nevis, Surinam, St. Vincent & the Grenadines, Trinidad & Tobago, Uruguay, USA Virgin Islands, and Venezuela.

Oceania – member nations 19:

American Samoa, Australia, Cook Islands, Federated States of Micronesia, Fiji, French Polynesia, Guam, Kiribati, Marshall Islands, Nauru, New Caledonia, New Zealand, Palau, Papua New Guinea, samoa, Solomon Islands, Tonga, Tuvalu, and Vanuatu.

Figure 4.4   WTF Regional Member Nations

KEY: Europe (1) Asia (2) Africa (3) Pan America (4) Oceania (5)

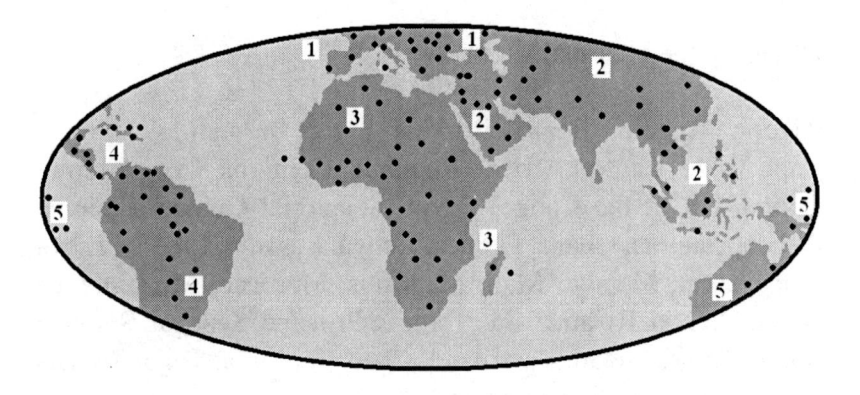

Olympic Sport

In terms of the number of member countries of International Sports Federations (IF), Taekwondo has become one of the world's most popular sporting activities. In only 40 years, Taekwondo is ranked number 8 of IF member countries of 26 Olympic Sports. As depicted in the table below (Table 4.1), Volleyball rates as the most popularly played sport. Considering the rapid growth in numbers of people participating in Taekwondo, it is estimated that, although Taekwondo is currently rated as the 8th most popularly ranked sport, it is likely to supersede other sports such as swimming, tennis and football.

Table 4.1   No. of International Federations (IF) Member Countries of 26 Olympic Sports

Sports of the Summer Olympic Games	No. of IF Member Countries
1 Volleyball	220
2 Table Tennis	215
3 Athletics	213
4 Basketball	213
5 Football	208
6 Tennis	207
7 Swimming	202
8 Taekwondo	200
9 Judo	198
10 Boxing	196
11 Weightlifting	187
12 Cycling	174
13 Badminton	168
14 Wrestling	168
15 Handball	167
16 Canoeing	153
17 Shooting	147
18 Archery	145
19 Fencing	143
20 Sailing	138
21 Gymnastics	137
22 Equestrian	133
23 Triathlon	131
24 Rowing	130
25 Hockey	127
26 Modern Pentathlon	99

The rapid growth and success that Taekwondo has experienced so far is quite remarkable. Compared to the competitive sport of football perhaps, there is still a lot more that Taekwondo can learn in terms of promotion of the sport. More countries are members of FIFA than any other international federation body. The fan base has a huge following that is on a global scale. Manchester United is probably the most famous football club in the world, due to its success and media coverage. Global support and interest can be seen at major competitions such as the World Cup. Football supporters from all over the world are seen wearing the shirts or colours of teams that they support. This can be despite having little or no knowledge about other details concerning the home country of that football club. There are more supporters wearing the Manchester United shirt in China than in Manchester, England. Supporting football may involve actively playing on the football field, shouting from the terraces or watching television in the comfort of home. Individual supporters may show interest at a local, national or world level. Wearing a football shirt represents a part of an individual's identity, reveals their group membership and predicts sets of cultural practice. Ownership creates a sense of belonging to a football club that is often on the other side of the world, ignoring boundaries and borders of local and national territories.

The number of Taekwondo practitioners around the world is huge, estimated at 100 million. Drawing in spectators at sporting events is an area that needs to be strengthened. Taekwondo competition sport has been criticised at times as lacking in excitement. Some competitors who are winning and fear that further physical engagement may result in their opponent gaining points, avoid physical exchanges to try and protect their lead. This can result in the production of defensive strategies, which are not so entertaining to watch. The WTF have revised the competition rules with the aim of making Taekwondo sport more dynamic, without compromising the safety of the players. One of the changes made was to reduce the size of the competition area, from 12 metres by

12 metres to 8 metres by 8 metres. This makes it more difficult for competitors to avoid physical engagement with their opponent. Increases in dynamic fighting within competitions could attract increased media attention and larger audiences at events. Athletes who win major competitions with the correct exposure could become global super-stars, attracting bigger crowds in a similar fashion to top-flight football stars. Taekwondo is well placed to build on the successes and popularity it has achieved in recent years, and so gain the status of a top-flight global sport. The total number of Taekwondo practitioners (based on memberships within the European, Asian, African, and Pan American and Oceania regions) is estimated at 70 million to 100 million. The number of Martial Art schools in the US is estimated at 26,007. More than half of these are Taekwondo clubs. The total number of practitioners in Korea is estimated at over 7 million.

Other Martial Arts Membership

The Japanese martial art Karate has a membership estimated at 23 million in 140 nations. The Chinese martial art Wushu has a membership estimated at 75 million practitioners in 121 nations. Although Wushu membership levels are similar to that of Taekwondo, the main concentration of practitioners is based in mainland China.

Training continues.

Chapter 5

Standardisation of basic actions

Stances, kicks, blocks and strikes

Taekwondo practitioners, professional and amateur, follow a similar path through the coloured belt and black belt grading system. Olympic champions and world-class athletes must attain the rank of black belt before they are permitted to take part in competitions at the highest level. The attainment of Kup grade or Dan grade status is not usually possible without being able to learn and demonstrate patterns. The World Taekwondo Headquarters provides and sets the technical standards that are required for Kup grade and Dan grade promotion tests. Adults and children are required to show a level of skill and understanding by demonstrating kicking and punching techniques in front of an examination board. Patterns form a major part of the two-stage grading curriculum.

Kicks, blocks, strikes and stances are taught within patterns. As practitioners advance through the grading system, more challenging defensive and offensive techniques are taught. Taekwondo practitioners do not use sticks or knives as weapons; instead, they train their muscles, joints and limbs to act as blocking and striking weapons. Muscular co-ordination is integrated with speed and power to defend oneself from an opponent's attack. Blocking actions such as knife-hand techniques, in the shape of an open-handed blade, and motions that use a clenched fist, inner and low blocks, must be executed to inflict damage to the opponent's limbs. The idea is to use the blocks as striking motions that would incapacitate an opponent's arms and legs so that they cannot continue their attack.

Striking actions are aimed at a variety of vital points on an opponent. The three main areas consist of high, middle and low sections. Punches are aimed at the philtrum (shallow vertical groove at the base of the nose) and the solar plexus (in the centre of the torso). Front kicks are delivered to the lower abdomen or groin. Practitioners are encouraged to strike hard and fast with accuracy, focus and commitment. It is imperative that these actions are well controlled when executed with force. Instructors monitor their students' progress towards gaining these skills. Techniques that are executed incorrectly or loosely with little control and accuracy could cause injury to the elbows, wrists or fingers.

Correct stances provide the practitioner with stability, a solid base in which to launch defensive and offensive actions. Power in the techniques comes from the lower abdomen, the hips or waist. Balance is a crucial factor that can impact on the degree of accuracy, speed and power. Poor balance can render a practitioner vulnerable to injury or falling when attacked. An awareness of the centre of gravity, the torso in relation to the placement of the feet on the floor, plays a crucial role in the delivery of any type of techniques employed. Foot positions vary; for instance, a walking stance is shorter than a forward stance. Walking stances allow for speedy, impulsive motions. However, the centre of balance is higher, which can make the stance more unstable and unable to absorb strong, powerful blows. Forward stances, where the feet are further apart, provide a lower centre of gravity, supporting powerful, hard blocking and striking actions. The design of the forward stance does not allow for speedy, agile movements in terms of changing the direction of travel. Various stances, kicking and blocking skills are learnt throughout the two-stage grading system. Expectations in terms of the performance, the degree of power, speed, focus and spirit are higher at Black belt grades. An appreciation of the basic movements, principles and values of Taekwondo are taught at Kup grade. Dan grades aim to improve and perfect the basic techniques through repetition. These are developed through the black belt patterns. Dan grades are expected and encouraged to perform patterns with more power, speed, focus and spirit compared to when they were a Kup grade.

Figure 5.1   Technical Training Curriculums (a, b, c, d)

(a) 10th, 9th and 8th Kup Training Curriculum

10th Kup White Belt	9th Kup Yellow Tag on White Belt	8th Kup Yellow Belt
Ready stance	High section punch	Inner block, punch, punch
Kihap (shout)	Inner knife-hand strike	Low section X block
Free sparring stance	Reverse outerform block	Back kick
Guarding block	Outer knife-hand strike	Inner crescent kick
Punch (middle, low, high)	Side horse riding stance	Outer crescent kick
Forward stance	Side back-fist strike	Skipping side kick
Low section block	High front kick	Jumping front kick
Outerform block	High side kick	Free sparring
Inner block	Inner chopping kick	Pre-arranged sparring

High section block	Outer chopping kick	Pattern No. 1
Raising kick	Turning kick	
Front and side kicks	45 degree roundhouse kick	
Kibon hand drill No. 1	Kibon leg drill No. 1	
Kibon hand drill No. 2	Kibon leg drill No. 2	

(b) 7th, 6th and 5th Kup Training Curriculum

7th Kup Green Tag on Yellow Belt	6th Kup Green Belt	5th Kup Blue Tag on Green Belt
Palm thrust strike	Back stance	Spear hand strike
Front backfist strike	Inner palm block	Downward palm block
Horizontal target elbow strike	Vertical punch	Jumping side kick
Reverse outer knife-hand block	Inner/outer crescent kick (same leg)	Knife-hand guarding block
Reinforced outerform block	360 degrees jumping inner crescent kick	Inner crescent block kick, (same leg) side kick
Skip in front kick	Front kick – breaking	Front hook kick
Skip in roundhouse kick	Pattern No. 3	Back hook kick
Low/high front kick		Side kick – breaking
Low/high turning kick		Kibon hand drill No. 3
Pattern No. 2		Pattern No. 4

(c) 4th, 3rd and 2nd Kup Training Curriculum

4th Kup Blue Belt	3rd Kup Red Tag on Blue Belt	2nd Kup Red Belt
Hammer-fist strike	Cat stance	Ridge hand strike
Jumping turning kick	Wedge block	Uppercut punch
180 degree outer crescent kick	Scissors block	Low/high back kick
180 degree outer chopping kick	Knee strike	Jumping back kick
Simultaneous high block, reverse middle punch	Checking front and side kicks	Jumping double front kick
Turning kick – breaking	Back hook kick – breaking	Flying side kick – breaking
Kibon hand drill No. 4	Kibon leg drill No. 3	Jumping spinning kick
Pattern No. 5	Pattern No. 6	Kibon leg drill No. 4
		Pattern No. 7

(d) 1st Kup and 1st Dan Training Curriculum, and Additional Techniques

1st Kup Black Tag on Red Belt	1st Dan Black Belt	Additional techniques (All grades)
Philosophy	Tiger mouth strike	Front hand jab (straight)
Half mountain block	Knee break	Front hand jab (vertical)

Mountain block	Twin outerform block	Hook punch (face/body)
Jumping back hook kick	Twin temple punch	Uppercut punch (chin/ribs)
Back hook kick/turning kick	Upper palm strike (groin)	Breakfalls
Low front kick, outer chopping kick (same leg)	Side kick, turning kick (same leg)	180 degree outer knife-hand strike
Front hook kick/turning kick (same leg)	Triple kicks – side/back kicks (low, middle, high)	180 degree side backfist strike
Back kick – breaking	'U'-shaped strike	Pushing kick
Pattern No. 8	Pattern – Koryo	Sweeping kicks

Training continues.

Chapter 6

Kibon hand and leg drills 1-4

Kibon hand and leg drills

Kibon drills are similar in structure to Taegeuk and Dan grade patterns. Techniques are executed at the same spot, moving forward, backward and to the left and right side. There are four hand drills and four leg drills. Each routine comprises of 8 movements. Practitioners must form a ready stance before starting the drills and on completion of the exercise. These routines assist the practitioner's development of speed, power, balance and muscular strength. In order to perform the drills effectively, powerfully and with the appearance of apparent ease, practitioners must work on flexibility, posture and co-ordination.

Note: The reverse hand (the arm which is not used to execute blocking or striking actions) is placed at the side of the waist with the palm facing up and applies to Kibon hand drills 1-4.

Kibon hand drill 1

Start: Ready stance, facing north.

1. Turn left 90° (move left foot), side horse riding stance, low block (West).
2. Stationary, turn the head right 180°, low block (East).
3. Stationary, turn the head left 180°, outerform block (West).
4. Stationary, turn the head right 180°, outerform block (East).
5. Stationary, turn the head left 90°, left hand high block (North).
6. Stationary, right hand high block (North).
7. Stationary, left hand middle punch (North).
8. Stationary, right hand middle punch (North) and kihap.

Fast hand movements are crucial to this routine. Techniques must be executed with large actions and lightning speed in order to generate power.

Kibon hand drill 2

Start: Ready stance, facing north.

1. Move left foot out to the side, horse riding stance, left inner block (North).
2. Stationary, right inner block (North).
3. Turn right 90° (move right foot), forward stance, left inner knife-hand strike (East).
4. Turn left 180° (move left foot), forward stance, right inner knife-hand strike (West).
5. Turn right 180° (pivot on the spot), forward stance, left low knife-hand block (position the block at the centre line of the body, protecting the groin, with the eyes looking North).
6. Turn left 180° (pivot on the spot), forward stance, right low knife-hand block (position the block at the centre line of the

body, protecting the groin, with the eyes looking North).
7. Turn right 90° (pivot on the spot), horse riding stance, left high punch (North).
8. Stationary, right high punch (North) and kihap.

Practitioners must twist or turn the hips with the techniques to generate power. Using the core of the body or waist combined with fast hand speed greatly enhances power.

Kibon hand drill 3

Start: Ready stance, facing north.

1. Turn left 90° (move left foot), back stance, knife-hand block (West).
2. Turn right 180° (move right foot), back stance, knife-hand block (East).
3. Turn left 180° (pivot on the spot), back stance, low knife-hand guarding block (West). On preparation the hands are positioned at the right side of the head.
4. Turn right 180° (pivot on the spot), back stance, low knife-hand guarding block (East). The block is performed with a large circular action, moving the hands across the body (to the right), then upwards and placed at the left side of the head, and completing the technique in a downward motion to the right side.
5. Turn left 180° (pivot on the spot), back stance, middle section knife-hand guarding block (West). On preparation the hands are positioned at the right side of the head.
6. Turn right 180° (pivot on the spot), back stance, middle section knife-hand guarding block (East). On preparation the hands are positioned at the left side of the head.
7. Turn left 90° (move the right foot across slightly), horse riding stance, right downward palm block, left vertical spear

hand strike towards the solar plexus (North). The right hand is placed underneath the left elbow.
8. Stationary, horse riding stance, left downward palm block, right vertical spear hand strike towards the solar plexus (North) and kihap. The left hand is placed underneath the right elbow.

This drill must be demonstrated with sharp, precise actions. Techniques must twist, tense and accelerate at the end of the motion with focused concentration. Practitioners must work at this drill to generate power.

Kibon hand drill 4

Start: Ready stance, facing north.

1. Move forward (move left foot), forward stance, vertical elbow strike.
2. Move backward (move the left foot behind the right foot), back stance, back thrust elbow strike (East). Place the right hand on the left fist.
3. Turn left 90° (draw the left foot up slightly), side horse riding stance, side thrust elbow strike (West). Place the right fist at the side of the waist.
4. Stationary (turn the head right 90°), left downward elbow strike (North).
5. Move forward (move right foot), forward stance, vertical elbow strike.
6. Move backward (move the right foot behind the left foot), back stance, back thrust elbow strike (West). Place the left hand on the right fist.
7. Turn right 90° (draw the right foot up slightly), side horse riding stance, side thrust elbow strike (East). Place the left fist at the side of the waist.

8. Stationary (turn the head left 90°), right downward elbow strike (North) and kihap.

Practitioners must keep the core of the body vertical to maintain a good posture or shape. This will help maintain balance throughout the routine, which incorporates a variety of stances that move forward, backward and to the side.

Kibon leg drill 1

Start: Ready stance, facing north.

1. Turn left 45° (move left foot), forward stance, twin low section block. Stationary, right leg raising kick and replace the foot behind, forward stance, twin low section block.
2. On the spot, right front kick and place the foot down next to the left foot, close stance, then step back with the left foot, forward stance, twin low section block.
3. Stationary, left leg raising kick and replace the foot behind, forward stance, twin low section block.
4. On the spot, left front kick and place the foot down next to the right foot, close stance, then turn right 90° (move the right foot), forward stance, twin low section block.
5. Stationary, left leg raising kick and replace the foot behind, forward stance, twin low section block.
6. On the spot, left front kick and place the foot down next to the right foot, close stance, then step back with the right foot, forward stance, twin low section block.
7. Stationary, right leg raising kick and replace the foot behind, forward stance, twin low section block.
8. On the spot, right front kick (Kihap) and place the foot down next to the left foot, close stance, then turn left 90° (move the left foot), forward stance, twin low section block.

Raising and front kicks must be executed with the core of the body in a vertical or slightly bent forward position, with the arms placed into a guarding block. Front kicks must be executed with the knee bent before and after the motion. Raising kicks can be demonstrated with the knee slightly bent or with the leg straight. Pivoting on the ball of the supporting foot, with the heel slightly raised off the floor enhances the speed of the kicking actions. The body weight must not rest on the entire sole of the supporting foot. Twin low section blocks on preparation, the forearms must cross over at chest height, if the left foot is placed in front (Step 1) then the left arm must be placed on the outside. The right arm is positioned on the inside - between the left arm and the body. If the right foot is placed in front (Step 2), the right arm is placed on the outside. The left arm is positioned on the inside, between the right arm and the body.

Kibon leg drill 2

Start: Ready stance, facing north.

1. Turn left 90° (move left foot), side horse riding stance, twin low section block. Move forward (move right foot in front) cross legged stance, left side leg raising kick (West), step down side horse riding stance and turn the head right 180°, twin low section block (East).
2. Move forward (move left foot in front), cross legged stance, right side leg raising kick (East), step down side horse riding stance and turn the head left 180°, twin low section block (West).
3. Move forward (move right foot in front) cross legged stance, left side kick (West), step down side horse riding stance and turn the head right 180°, twin low section block (East).
4. Move forward (move left foot in front) cross legged stance, right side kick (East), step down side horse riding stance and

turn the head left 180°, twin low section block (West).
5. Move forward, right side kick (West), side horse riding stance, twin low section block.
6. Move forward, left low/high side kick (West), step down side horse riding stance and turn the head right 180°, twin low section block (East).
7. Move forward, left side kick (East), side horse riding stance, twin low section block.
8. Move forward, right low/high side kick (East) and kihap, step down side horse riding stance and turn the head left 180°, twin low section block (West).

Practitioners must pay attention to detail when demonstrating the side kick. The body must be turned side on when the side kick is executed, with the arms placed in front of the chest. The supporting foot must turn so that the toes are pointing in the opposite direction to the kick. The head must turn with the eyes looking over the shoulder, focused on the target. Practitioners must ensure that the height of the kicks is kept within their capability to ensure good posture or shape, balance and power.

Kibon leg drill 3

Start: Ready stance, facing north.

1. Turn left 90° (move left foot), back stance, guarding block. Move forward, front kick, back stance, guarding block (West).
2. Move forward, roundhouse kick (West), step down in front and turn right 180°, back stance, guarding block (East).
3. Move forward, front kick, back stance, guarding block (East).
4. Move forward, roundhouse kick (East), step down in front and turn left 180°, back stance, guarding block (West).
5. Move forward, right leg roundhouse kick and land in front, back stance, then left leg back hook kick and step down after

spinning 360°, into the same back stance, guarding block (West).
6. Move forward, roundhouse kick (West), step down in front and turn right 180°, back stance, guarding block (East).
7. Move forward, left leg roundhouse kick and land in front, back stance, then right leg back hook kick and step down after spinning 360°, into the same back stance, guarding block (East).
8. Move forward, roundhouse kick (East) and kihap, step down in front and turn left 180°, back stance, guarding block (West).

This drill must be demonstrated with good balance, accuracy, speed and control. Good flexibility assists practitioners in the performance of this drill. Steps 1 and 2 can be performed continuously without stopping. Steps 3 and 4 can be performed continuously without stopping.

Kibon leg drill 4

Start: Ready stance, facing north.

1. Stationary, left jumping front kick (North).
2. Stationary, right jumping front kick (North).
3. Stationary, double jumping front kick, with both feet close together (North).
4. Stationary, double jumping front kick, with both feet out to the sides (North).
5. Stationary, left jumping side kick (West).
6. Stationary, right jumping side kick (East).
7. Turn right 90°, left jumping roundhouse kick (East), and return to ready stance (facing north).
8. Turn left 90°, right jumping roundhouse kick (West) and kihap, and return to ready stance (facing north).

This drill demands physical strength, flexibility and determination. Good muscle strength and agility assist in executing jumping techniques swiftly. Practitioners must have the endurance to demonstrate the routine in one continuous sequence.

Training continues.

Chapter 7

Fuel for the mind and body

Dietary intake and physical performance

The goal of professional athletes is to achieve their full potential. The ultimate aim is to out-perform everyone else in their category, in pursuit of the top prize. Performance at the highest level requires athletes to adhere to rigid training schedules. Regular monitoring of health, fitness, physical and mental strength, nutrition, hydration and sleep patterns form part of the strategy. These regimes become part of the athlete's lifestyle. Nutritional status plays a vital role in assisting athletes to meet the demands of their sport, and to produce the best possible performance.

Chemical reactions that underlie all physiological processes require fuel. The entire human body is made up of chemical substances that are continuously interacting with one another. Fuel or energy is used for all bodily functions, such as skeletal movements, digestion, the pumping of the heart, mental activity and planning, including ideas and thoughts. The fuel that the body needs is gained through dietary intake. Nutrients obtained from food assist normal growth, maintenance and repair. Some nutrients are converted by the body into cellular energy. There are four major nutrients. These nutrients can be commonly found in food.

Table 7.1 Nutrients and function

Major Nutrients	Main Functions
Carbohydrates	Converted into glucose and used as cellular energy.
Lipids	Converted into stored energy and also forms a structural protective membrane around cells.
Proteins	Assists tissue maintenance and growth.
Water	Assists the digestion process and provides the body with an efficient cooling mechanism. Perspiration is mostly water.

Fuel for the mind and body

Capacity to complete work is contingent upon the consumption of 'fuel' and the resulting generation of power. The more demanding a task is, the higher the demands are for 'fuel'. Applying oneself to a physical exercise or task uses more energy than 'going through the motions'. Taekwondo practitioners, for example, are encouraged to show commitment and spirit when demonstrating patterns. The motions must be executed with speed and power, requiring physical and mental energy. Practitioners expel more energy demonstrating advanced coloured belt patterns compared with coloured belt pattern number 1, which consists of fewer movements and basic actions.

The body's major fuel is glucose, which is a type of sugar, monosaccharide. The body is able to break down glucose fuel molecules inside cells, releasing stored energy. Most cells within the body can only use a few simple sugars that the body needs to sustain life. Glucose is at the top of the cellular menu. Glucose is converted from foods that contain carbohydrates. These are mostly in the form of starches and are absorbed or released as energy. The conversion process begins in the mouth. Salivary amylase is present in saliva and acts to split starch into smaller fragments of monosaccharide. When the food enters the stomach, the conversion process is continued by the stomach's protein-digesting enzymes. Carbohydrates are broken down to their chemical building blocks (monomers). At this stage they are small enough to be absorbed and provide the body with an easy, ready source of cellular fuel. Used energy is replenished when the next meal arrives.

The body needs other substances such as lipid fats and proteins to sustain life and assist development. These substances, including glucose, circulate around the body in the bloodstream. Blood flow is the common transport pool that provides cellular energy and is drawn on by all the body cells. The brain is unique, as it is protected by a blood-brain barrier that prevents many substances found in the bloodstream from entering its domain. Proteins, bacteria, viruses, certain toxins and most drugs are restricted. This is to ensure that the brain has control of its microenvironment and is not influenced by unwanted chemical reactions. The main source of fuel to the brain is glucose, which can pass through the protective barrier. Unlike the rest of the body, the brain cannot obtain its energy from fats. Type of dietary intake has a direct effect on the physical material body and the intellectual emotional responses of the mind.

- The body requires a variety of foods for fuel in the form of glucose, fats, proteins and vitamins, which assist in the performance of physical exercise.

- The brain is fuelled mainly by glucose, which is converted from carbohydrates. Mental exercises that involve focus, planning and ideas are an emergent property of the brain. Skeletal, muscular movements are controlled by the brain at a conscious and unconscious level.

- A variety of nutrients is vital for maintenance, development and growth of a healthy mind and body.

Figure 7.1   Carbohydrates dietary sources

Complex Carbohydrates (Starches)	**Simple Carbohydrates (Sugars)**	**Complex and Simple Carbohydrates**
Bread	Carbonated Drinks	Pastries
Cereal	Sweets	Pies
Crackers	Fruit	Biscuits
Flour	Sugar cane	Cakes
Pasta	Sugar beet	
Nuts	Honey	
Grains	Milk	
Potatoes	Ice-cream	
Legumes (Beans, peas)	Pudding	
Root vegetables	Young (immature) vegetables	

Good nutritional intake leads to optimal performance and long-term benefits. The daily amount of carbohydrate recommended is 125 to 175 grams. See Appendix 7.1, illustrating various kinds of food and their carbohydrate content which, once consumed and converted into glucose, the body and mind can use for fuel.

- Excess consumption of complex carbohydrates can lead to

obesity.
- Eating sugary foods instead of more complex carbohydrates, such as replacing milk with carbonated drinks or replacing wholegrain bread with biscuits, may cause nutritional deficiencies as well as obesity.
- Avoid foods that are low in nutrients and high in saturated fats and sugars.

Figure 7.2   Recommended dietary and exercise guidelines

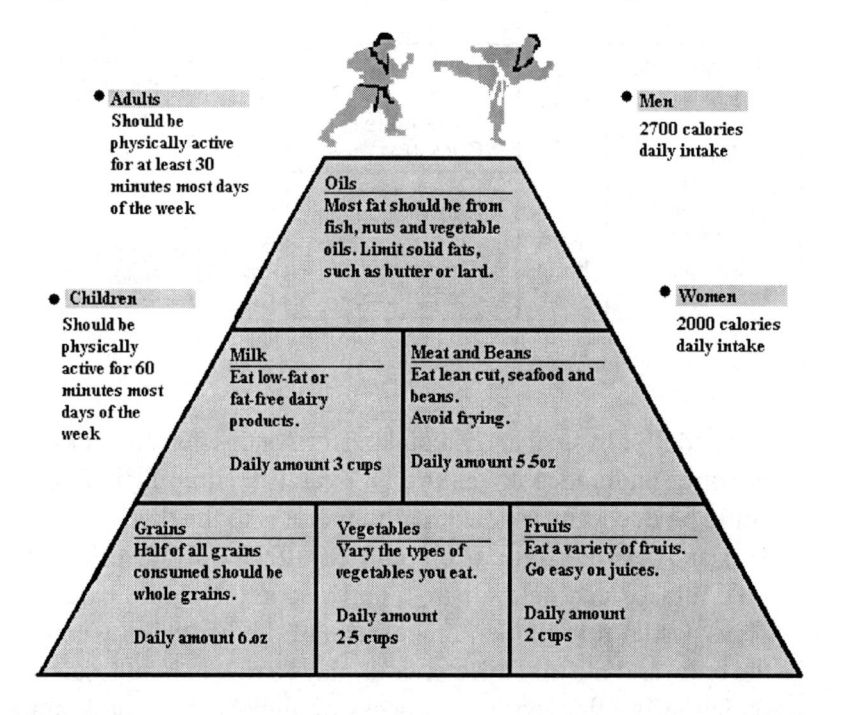

- **Adults** Should be physically active for at least 30 minutes most days of the week
- **Children** Should be physically active for 60 minutes most days of the week
- **Men** 2700 calories daily intake
- **Women** 2000 calories daily intake

Oils Most fat should be from fish, nuts and vegetable oils. Limit solid fats, such as butter or lard.

Milk Eat low-fat or fat-free dairy products. Daily amount 3 cups

Meat and Beans Eat lean cut, seafood and beans. Avoid frying. Daily amount 5.5oz

Grains Half of all grains consumed should be whole grains. Daily amount 6.oz

Vegetables Vary the types of vegetables you eat. Daily amount 2.5 cups

Fruits Eat a variety of fruits. Go easy on juices. Daily amount 2 cups

Performance

Without appropriate nutritional intake, the full potential of athletes will not be realised. Performance will not be at its peak and training levels may not be sustained. Dietary regimens that take into account the type and quantity of fluid and food consumed can help to combat fatigue that is associated with decreased performance. Fatigue could be the result of an inadequate quantity of carbohydrates. Decreased performance could be the result of dehydration. Appropriate nutritional intake aids endurance, speed, agility, mobility and strength.

Figure 7.3   Performance, nutrition and hydration

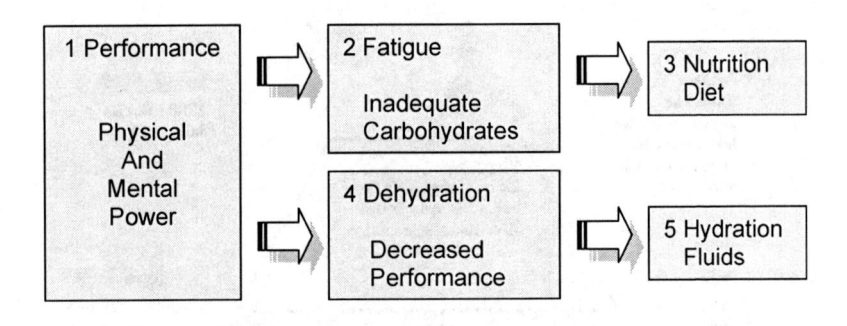

```
┌─────────────────┐     ┌─────────────────┐     ┌─────────────────┐
│ 1 Performance   │     │ 2 Fatigue       │     │ 3 Nutrition     │
│                 │ ──▶ │                 │ ──▶ │   Diet          │
│   Physical      │     │   Inadequate    │     └─────────────────┘
│     And         │     │   Carbohydrates │
│   Mental        │     ├─────────────────┤     ┌─────────────────┐
│   Power         │     │ 4 Dehydration   │     │ 5 Hydration     │
│                 │ ──▶ │                 │ ──▶ │   Fluids        │
│                 │     │   Decreased     │     └─────────────────┘
│                 │     │   Performance   │
└─────────────────┘     └─────────────────┘
```

- 1, 2 and 3   Physical and mental performances that are lacking in spirit, endurance or feature an overall feeling of tiredness could be due to insufficient carbohydrates in the diet.
- 1, 4 and 5   Performance could be affected by insufficient fluid intake, leading to distress and discomfort. Fluid balance plays a vital role in the homeostasis of the body, influencing the body and the mind. Behaviour plays a role in homeostasis. Satiation is achieved by a process of signals from the brain, providing motivation to act, to preserve energy and search for fluids. Dehydration can be avoided by drinking before, during and after physical exercise.

Recovery and repair

Impaired nutritional status is implicated in depressing immune responses and depleting endurance levels. Susceptibility to infections and injuries increases. There are associated delays in recovery time. Appropriate nutritional status speeds up recovery. In turn, the body becomes stronger, fitter. An improvement in overall health allows athletes to lengthen and intensify training sessions.

Figure 7.4   Recovery and repair

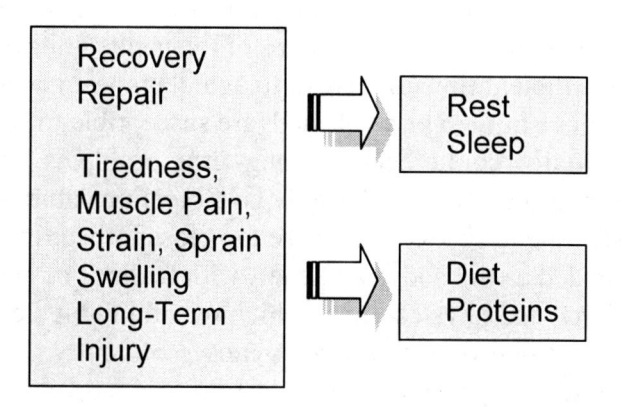

Recovery Repair — Tiredness, Muscle Pain, Strain, Sprain Swelling Long-Term Injury	⇨	Rest Sleep
	⇨	Diet Proteins

- Recovery and repair of the body and mind after physical and mental exercise draws on foods that provide nutrients, proteins and vitamins. Appropriate levels of rest and sleep have a crucial role in the healing and recovery process.

One of the most underestimated natural aids to recovery is regular, solid sleep. The amount and quality of sleep directly impacts on wellbeing. Appropriate and quality sleep enhances recovery from muscle and other types of discomfort, pain and fatigue. Usually 8 to 9 hours sleep allows appropriate time for tissue repair and to wake up in the morning feeling relaxed and refreshed.

Injuries are more likely to occur during performances when the body is overtired or an insufficient warm-up and cool-down routine has been adopted. Warm-up exercises play a crucial role in the prevention of injuries. Warm-ups circulate the flow of blood, increasing the muscle's ability to stretch, reducing the possibility of sudden, awkward or over exertive motions that could lead to strains and sprains. Strains, torn muscle fibres, often leave the muscle feeling tight after exercise or tend to cramp. Sprains occur when the ligaments holding the bones in place are overstretched or torn. The blood supply to ligaments is poor and impacts on the time taken to heal. Since the supply of nutrients and proteins is restricted, rest and sleep are crucial factors that assist the healing process of ligaments. Injuries must be given sufficient time to recover to avoid a repeat occurrence. Muscles, once injured or weakened, are susceptible to re-injury and potentially could become long-term problems. Regular exercise promotes sleep as the body is left feeling naturally tired and needs time to recover. Exercise too close to bed time is not recommended as the body can be left with feelings of euphoria, an emotional and physical high, which would inhibit sleep.

Fatigue is one of the principle causes of injury. Complex carbohydrates provide long-lasting energy. Simple carbohydrates offer a quick, short supply of energy. To combat fatigue, particularly when endurance is needed, long sugars are recommended in the diet. A major cause of fatigue can be associated with dietary intake. Milk, animal protein and fats are difficult to break down and digest. The body has to use more energy for digestion and assimilation. In a broad sense, excessive consumption of certain foods is unhelpful to overall health or performance. Some types of food have particular nutritional values and are useful in assisting the healing processes of connective tissues. Muscles and joints are comprised of connective tissue. The links between types of foods consumed, sleep patterns, exercise, recovery and repair have been well researched. An understanding of these areas is necessary if optimal health and wellbeing are to be realised.

Figure 7.5   Foods to avoid in excessive amounts.

Avoid excessive consumption	Possible implications
Red meat, Cheese, Pork chops, Fried foods, Whole milk, Butter or margarine	Probable risk factor for injuries. Excess calories that could lead to obesity
Salt	Impairs wound healing
Caffeine	Reduces blood supply by narrowing blood vessels. Reduces nutrient supply
Fast foods (contains fat, salt and sugar)	Deficient in vitamins and minerals. May lead to muscle pulls or cramps
White sugar, honey (simple sugars)	Can increase the pain of injuries

Figure 7.6   Foods that assist healing.

Assists the body to heal	Promotes
Oatmeal with added wheat germ	Helps to prevents strains and aids healing
Oats	Supports connective tissue formation
Fresh fruit, raw juices, vegetables	Offsets the negative effects of acidic waste that builds up during exercise
Cheese and yeast	Helps the body to use glucose more efficiently during exercise, which reduces the risk of possible strains and sprains

Berries, broccoli, cantaloupe, mangoes, dark leafy greens	Assists repair of connective tissue and reduce inflammation
Sprouts, avocadoes, whole grains, legumes, nuts, seeds, dark leafy vegetables	Nutrients for connective tissue and cell repair. Helps prevent internal scarring
Fish oils, green and yellow fruits, vegetables	Nutrients for connective tissue and cell repair
Fresh organic oils; flax, seed, hemp, olive	Important for tissue elasticity, muscle flexibility, joint motion, regulating inflammatory response
Fresh pineapple	Combats swelling and pain after an injury, helps the healing process by breaking down the injured tissue
Fish, fowl, lamb	Good source of protein

An example of a healthy diet

It is important for all individuals to eat correctly in order to improve health, energy levels and the ability to fight off disease. A healthy diet provides a balanced intake of energy and nutrients. Eating for general health, to lose weight or gain muscle, requires the same diet. When aiming to lose weight, the energy gained from food should be burned off with exercise; this promotes weight loss. Athletes need to be aware that inclusions of the wrong foods in their diet can hinder the muscle-building process. Muscles built on vegetables and fruit will grow strong; muscles built on burgers and chips will grow fat. The amount of calories should be increased to compensate for higher activity level.

    A calorie chart can be used to find preferred foods for inclusion in a weekly diet. A sample, seven-day menu can be found below, based on 1500 calories per day, and contains all the nutrients needed in a diet. Small snacks can be eaten in between meals to prevent feelings of hunger, which can include sandwiches, sausage rolls, rice pudding and an occasional cake or bar of chocolate. Avoid increasing the size of main meals.

This chart can be adjusted to suit an individual's preferences and varied from one week to the next, to relieve boredom. All meat products can be substituted with vegetarian alternatives such as pasta, rice or jacket potato.

Day 1

Breakfast	Lunch	Dinner
1 orange 1 boiled egg 1 slice multigrain bread 2 tsp low-fat spread	Tuna fish 90g Salad: lettuce, onions and 1 tomato. 2 celery sticks Beetroot 2 tsp mayonnaise 2 crispbreads 1 apple	Chicken casserole: Chicken, skinless 90g, carrots, onions, parsnips and turnips. Jacket potato 80g Unsalted green beans 1 pear

Day 2

Breakfast	Lunch	Dinner
Half grapefruit Bran flakes Natural yogurt 75ml	1 slice extra lean ham Mixed bean salad 1 tsp chopped parsley Chopped spring onions 1 cup shredded iceberg lettuce 1 tomato Cucumber 2 sticks celery 1 tsp vegetable oil 1 medium slice melon	Homemade soup: 1 stock cube, celery, onion and carrot. Steamed or baked white fish in white sauce. Green beans 1 tsp margarine 1 baked apple

Day 3

Breakfast	Lunch	Dinner
1 cup unsweetened orange or grapefruit juice. Drained sardines 1 slice multi/ wholegrain brown bread. 2 tsp low-fat spread 1 tomato	2 crispbread Cottage cheese Salad: 1 tomato, celery, cucumber, grated carrot, shredded cabbage, onion and red pepper. 2 tsp low-fat spread/cheese 1 banana	Sautéed onion in 1 tsp vegetable oil with liver. Cooked long-grain brown rice Spinach 1 tomato Mushrooms Mango sliced Natural yogurt 75ml

Day 4

Breakfast	Lunch	Dinner
Red or green grapes Scrambled eggs 1 tomato 1 slice multi/ wholegrain brown bread. 2 tsp low-fat spread	Macaroni cheese: Grated cheese mixed with mushrooms, cauliflower and skimmed milk. Iceberg lettuce, spring onion, cucumber and grated carrot. 1 orange	Mackerel Potato Peas Carrots 1 apple

Day 5

Breakfast	Lunch	Dinner
Stewed prunes with their juice (no sugar in juice). Muesli Natural yogurt 75ml	Baked beans - unsalted 1 poached egg 1 slice multi/ wholegrain brown bread. 2 tsp low-fat spread Salad: grated cabbage, onion, carrot, celery and pepper. Pineapple	1 fillet salmon – fresh Cucumber Corn on the cob Green beans Pepper Low-fat spread 1 orange

Day 6

Breakfast	Lunch	Dinner
Half grapefruit 1 poached egg 1 tomato Mushrooms 1 slice multi/ wholegrain brown bread. 2 tsp low-fat spread	Jacket potato with boiled shrimps, chopped parsley and 1 tblsp mayonnaise. Salad: iceberg lettuce, celery, cucumber, pepper and spring onions. 1 pear	Roast turkey – skinless Pasta with peas, celery, spring onion, spinach, blackcurrants and 1 tsp vegetable oil. Natural yogurt 75ml

Day 7

Breakfast	Lunch	Dinner
Pineapple Porridge Skimmed milk 1 tblsp honey	Lean beef Baked jacket potato 2 tsp low-fat spread Broccoli Carrots Boiled parsnips Natural yogurt 75ml	Pilchards in tomato sauce. Salad: lettuce, tomato, celery, cucumber and peppers. 3 crispbread 2 tsp low-fat cheese 2 plums

Harmonisation

Harmonisation is a constant cycle of events, designed to maintain balance within the system and lead to feelings of good health, energy and spirit. A general sense of well-being is linked with a dietary regimen that provides appropriate amounts and types of nutrients. Cellular fuel is used to sustain life and assist in the development and maintenance of physical and mental power. Appropriate levels of sleep and rest must be incorporated into the lifestyle, together with the replenishing of nutrients for the successful healing of tired, exhausted muscle groups within the body.

An active lifestyle, physical exercise, combined with an appropriate diet promotes a healthy mind and body. Dietary intake impacts upon the physical and mental energy available to sustain life and to perform physical exercise. Adequate warm-up and cool-down exercises help to prevent injuries. Physical and mental fitness are associated with a healthy immune system, the ability to fall asleep easily at night, sleeping well, feeling refreshed in the mornings and an overall sense of generally feeling healthy.

Figure 7.7 Physical and mental development, performance and recovery

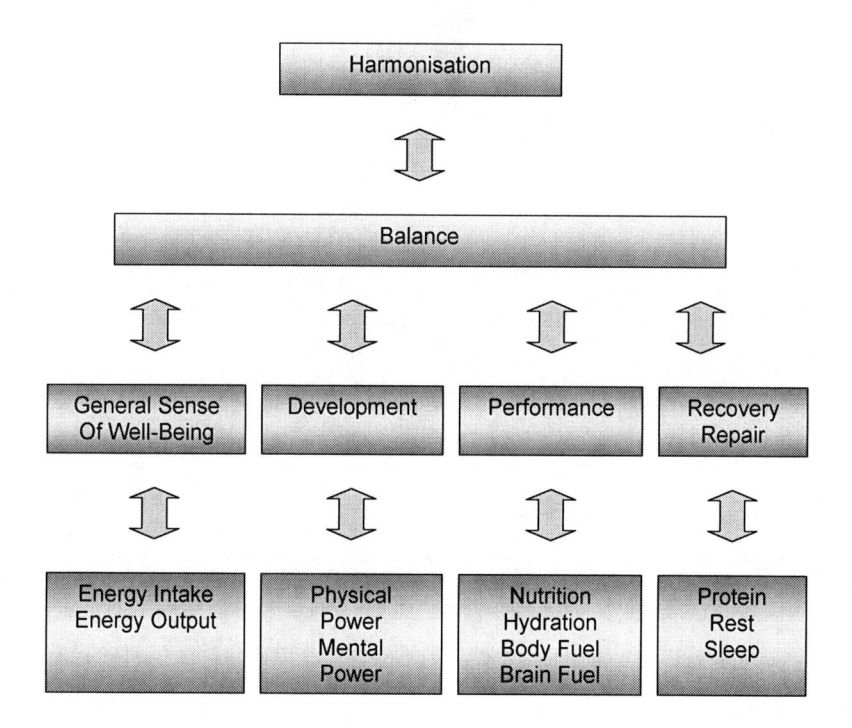

```
                    ┌──────────────────┐
                    │  Harmonisation   │
                    └──────────────────┘
                             ⇅
        ┌──────────────────────────────────────────┐
        │                Balance                    │
        └──────────────────────────────────────────┘
           ⇅            ⇅            ⇅            ⇅
   ┌────────────┐ ┌───────────┐ ┌───────────┐ ┌───────────┐
   │General Sense│ │Development│ │Performance│ │ Recovery  │
   │Of Well-Being│ │           │ │           │ │  Repair   │
   └────────────┘ └───────────┘ └───────────┘ └───────────┘
         ⇅            ⇅              ⇅            ⇅
   ┌────────────┐ ┌───────────┐ ┌───────────┐ ┌───────────┐
   │Energy Intake│ │ Physical  │ │ Nutrition │ │  Protein  │
   │Energy Output│ │  Power    │ │ Hydration │ │   Rest    │
   │            │ │  Mental   │ │ Body Fuel │ │   Sleep   │
   │            │ │  Power    │ │ Brain Fuel│ │           │
   └────────────┘ └───────────┘ └───────────┘ └───────────┘
```

Reflection

I have found that regular routines incorporating training, diet, sleep and rest can greatly enhance overall fitness and performance. My daily lifestyle, mainly due to work commitments, changed from one week to the next. This prevented me from establishing regular routines. I soon realised that, no matter how hard I trained,

I could never quite achieve the same level of fitness as those whose routine was consistent from one week to the next. I had to be aware of these constraints and not allow them to detract from my general fitness, performance and progress.

Training continues.

Chapter 8

Understanding Patterns

Patterns

Patterns or poomsae, sometimes written as poomse, play a crucial role in the structure and education of the martial art. The routines incorporate principles and values that underpin Taekwondo practice. Physical and spiritual strength is developed through the actions and movements practised during the performance of poomsae. Each form is interwoven with its own philosophy that furthers development of the body and mind. Patterns are learnt over a period of many years. They progress in difficulty and complexity. Patterns are taught in accordance with obligatory time scales that are associated with the age of the practitioner. This reflects maturity in the sense of the length of time that practitioners have trained in Taekwondo and a presumed level of understanding. Practitioners learn patterns and aim to demonstrate them with perfect, accurate defensive and offensive techniques. Once appropriate levels of speed and power are achieved within the demonstration of patterns, testing for promotion is possible. Practitioners earn their promotion through repetition, hard work and commitment. This is part of the journey that Taekwondo practitioners undertake. Patterns continue to play a central role within the martial art. Without patterns, Taekwondo education would not be possible. Patterns remain at the heart of Taekwondo.

Sequenced movements within patterns consist of techniques executed with the hands and feet. Practitioners demonstrate actions with a specific purpose in mind, defending and attacking vital points of the body such as the solar plexus, against an imaginary opponent or opponents from any direction. Sparring is a practical application of patterns. Patterns travel along imaginary cardinal and intercardinal lines and frequently change direction (see chapter 1). The choreographed routines are not just put together randomly. Combinations of movements or the design of each pattern is planned and influenced by the attached philosophy. Coloured belt patterns favour physical development. Black belt patterns encourage development of spiritual strength (see chapter 1, 'developmental stages', paragraph 4). The fighting spirit of Taekwondo is manifested or expressed in the actions of patterns. Patterns can be practised in isolation, in the gymnasium or at a place of residence, without the presence of an instructor. In order to improve, refine the techniques, generating more speed and power, smoother and sharper motions, the support and guidance of a qualified instructor is invaluable.

Patterns that are practised today are the result of adaptations and developments applied using the knowledge and expertise of past generations to inform current practice. To standardise Taekwondo on a global scale, the World Taekwondo Headquarters (Kukkiwon) and the World Taekwondo Federation (WTF) require all practitioners to learn and progress through the coloured belt and black belt patterns. Coloured belt patterns are known as Taegeuk forms or Taegeuk poomsae. Promotion in the martial art is not possible without the knowledge of Taegeuk patterns and black belt patterns. Throughout the history of Taekwondo, other forms have been practised to further the development of the Korean martial art, such as Pal Gwe forms. Since the introduction of the Taegeuk patterns, all other forms except the black belt forms have become obsolete, including the Pal Gwe forms. The

Taegeuk symbol is probably most recognised by the name 'Yin Yang', which is displayed on the South Korean flag.

Figure 8.1　South Korean flag. The Yin Yang symbol is shown at the centre of the flag

Taegeuk means 'no beginning, no ending'. Tae means 'big' and geuk means 'eternity', which refers to infinity, timelessness and without limits. In a sense, a circle has no beginning and no end. The Taegeuk symbol represents a continuous movement of two forces, 'Yin' and 'Yang', within infinity, which merge as one. They are not in opposition to one another, but merge and change; for example, day transforms into night and night transforms into day. The relationship between yin and yang represents a balance, interdependence and interconnectedness of all things in the natural world. Patterns offer an example of the interplay that exists between two oppositional forces. Taekwondo practitioners constantly demonstrate and change between defensive (act in response) and offensive (make the first move) actions. Techniques are executed moving forward, backward and side to side. Kicking and punching techniques within patterns are executed within a state of equilibrium; for example, the action of launching a middle section punch from the side of the waist shares the same qualities as a pushing motion. When the punch is thrown, simultaneously the fist of the non-punching arm is retracted back to the side of the waist and is comparable to a pulling action. Both forces are separate and oppositional, which merge and replace one another. Yin becomes Yang and Yang becomes Yin. Yin is linked with things that are, for example, slowing, soft, dark, cold, wet, passive, yielding, and negative and pulls. In contrast, yang is linked with things that are fast, hard, bright, hot, dry, aggressive, firm, and positive and pushes. Yin is feminine, yang is masculine.

Aims

A Taekwondo practitioner's demonstration of successive rapid movements against imaginary multiple attacks can be divided into a performance that expresses physical and mental skills. Physical abilities comprise of speed, power, accuracy, balance, flexibility and fitness. Mental abilities are concerned with focus, concentration, enthusiasm and the Taekwondo spirit, which includes manner, etiquette and courtesy. Performances can be judged to express good flexibility and balance, but lack in spirit and commitment. In contrast, other performances can be observed to lack flexibility, balance and accuracy, but are powerful, enthusiastic and high spirited. The aim is to deliver a performance which is controlled, purposeful and confident, revealing a balanced understanding of physical and mental power.

Consciousness

Part of the process that leads to the development of power is the ability to demonstrate a pattern without conscious thought. Without paying direct attention to the activity in the sense of thinking about what technique comes next in the routine. Subjective decision-making through repetition becomes automatic, below the level of consciousness. Practitioners must aim to demonstrate patterns to the best of their ability. Strong, inspiring performances are more than just technically correct. Patterns must contain, visibly, appropriate levels of power, timing and meaning. Once patterns are familiar to the extent that a performance requires little or no conscious attention - power, rhythm and timing will be enhanced. Once a pattern is learnt habitually, less energy is exerted in motor co-ordination. The basic actions are performed automatically, beneath conscious awareness. Expenditure of nervous and muscular fuel is reduced. However, expert performers can still make mistakes. Absentmindedness, slips of habit can still occur. Practitioners should not be over-concerned, as mistakes will inevitably happen; this is just part of the process.

Performances: the self

Upon entering the Taekwondo gymnasium, practitioners automatically take on a role that requires certain attributes. Practitioners are expected to act out their role and perform duties that are appropriate for their status. Appearances inform others of individual status or social role; for example, the colour of the belt worn around the waist indicates rank within Taekwondo. Performances can be, in part, for private gain, or for the good of others. The duties of Kup grades are concerned with acting in an appropriate respectful manner and obeying the commands of instructors. Personal development is the underlying motive behind the Kup grade performance. Dan grade instructor's performances are in part aimed at the community, to teach the Korean martial art. The instructor's role involves being in charge of classes and exerting authority according to the level of status that they have achieved. Performances should encompass characteristics of self-belief and self-confidence, acting according to the audiences' expectations and demands. Thus, Taekwondo becomes part of an individual's character and identity.

Applying oneself

Applying oneself is a mental and physical act of attending to a task with concentration and focus. Applying oneself to a pattern or exercise is crucial in gaining personal development within the martial art. Pattern work provides a valuable tool in enhancing cardiovascular fitness. Executing techniques with speed, power and focus increases the heart rate and breathing rate. Executed with concentration and focus, pattern exercises are hard work, drawing on physical and mental energy. Practitioners demonstrating a pattern must learn how to deliver motions with power using the entire body. Physical and mental power, muscular co-ordination and concentration of the mind should be utilised to maximum effect and proficiency. Performances that lack appropriate application fail to develop the individual mentally and physically.

Competition

Performances of the highest standards require mental and physical strength. Competitors often have more success providing that:

- Flexibility is good, enabling high kicks to be performed easily whilst maintaining balance.
- Good muscle strength assists jumping kicks to be executed smoothly.
- Agility assists in the delivery of swift controlled actions.
- Endurance is vital in order to sustain powerful motions throughout the whole exercise.

Practitioners must consider and be aware that:

- Performances are enhanced with regular training and experience.
- Regular, repetitive practice enhances the refinement of techniques.
- Experience reduces the possibility of mistakes. This also enhances confidence.

Overall, good performances are judged to include a proper order and accuracy of techniques. Movements are connected with grace, rhythm and timing. Footwork is proficient, patterns start and finish at the same spot. Motions are executed with control, focus, speed and power. Experienced competitors apply themselves to performances demonstrating enthusiasm, determination, confidence and spirit. A competitor with a strong presence on the mat commands the attention of the audience.

Figure 8.2   Judging criteria for patterns

1.	**Correctness of pattern**	Proper order of techniques. Correct foot/hand shapes; for example, blade of foot on side kicks. Accuracy. No major mistakes. No restarting or failure to complete pattern.
2.	**Start and finish at the same spot**	Patterns must start and finish at the same spot. Proficiency of footwork and stances. Direction of travel is correct.
3.	**Eye control**	Head turns, looking in the direction of travel. Good concentration and focus.

4. Power and speed	Correct respiration, breathing control. Graceful, rhythm and timing, speed control. Good balance, no hesitation. Appropriate levels of low/high speed and strong/soft force. Neat, tidy and sharp movements.
5. Spirit	Competition manner, etiquette, attitude, determination, enthusiasm and commitment. Strong kihap (yell: a sound made simultaneously with the execution of a technique), appropriate number of and placement. Overall appearance, demonstrating a pattern with the inclusion of the characteristics, philosophy and meaning attached to that pattern.

Focused concentration

The outcome of a competition where both entrants attract similar marks may be determined by more abstract criteria. The competitor who demonstrates mental strength will have an advantage. Competitors who are appropriately confident in their own ability, focused and determined will ultimately achieve victory. When competitors are physically matched in terms of shape, skill and appearance, the deciding factor will be spiritual strength, the greater willpower to win. Mental strength is cultivated through the principle of change and movement. By applying oneself to physical activities, over time, mental efficiency is enhanced. Spiritual power controls physical actions through our thoughts and ideas. Behaviour, motivation or purpose is a physiological process that highlights the close relationship of the mind and body. Decision-making, degree of speed and power, timing and rhythm are controlled by the mind.

Active meditation

Physical development alone will not produce the best possible results. Practitioners should aim to develop mentally as well as physically. A firm belief in victory, self-reliance with clear objectives will increase the possibility of success. Performances must be in keeping with the individual's body structure and capabilities. The demonstration must incorporate mental endurance, courage and confidence. Competition performances require special attention. A practitioner's performance must be rehearsed and prepared before entering the competition. Patterns must be performed in the mind, without actual physical movements. Imagination is required to construct the application of techniques, to reinforce the knowledge of the patterns. The whole routine must be practised in the mind with focused concentration, drawing on mental power and blocking out all other thoughts. Practitioners must concentrate the spirit fully on the task in hand. Intrusive random thoughts disrupt mental concentration and impact negatively on the efficiency and power of performances. This type of mental preparation can be described as active meditation; unlike static meditation, where the mind is clear of thoughts and the body is still. Mental rehearsal of a pattern before the physical performance takes place keeps the task fresh in the mind, boosts confidence and assists the practitioner in performing to their maximum potential.

Training continues.

Chapter 9

Taegeuk Patterns 1-8
Composition and philosophy

Composition

Education in Taekwondo requires practitioners to thoroughly learn the coloured belt patterns before progressing on to the black belt forms. This is important as the attainment of a black belt also means instructor (see chapter 1). Practitioners at this level of attainment are expected to assist lower grades with their patterns. Basic understandings of the composition of the patterns ensure that standards are maintained and improved. Taegeuk poomsae contain basic actions that are easier to perform compared to the black belt forms. The Taegeuk series of patterns favour development of physical strength. Dan grade patterns are technically more complex and focus on the development of spiritual strength or inner strength by means of controlling the respiration. It is important to learn all the coloured belt forms to gain experience and have an understanding of the principles and values of Taekwondo before attempting the black belt forms. Actions within patterns alternate between defensive and offensive techniques and vary in terms of favouring hand or foot techniques, and the degree of speed and power applied.

Composition 1: Hand and foot techniques

- Favours hand techniques.
- Favours foot techniques.
- Balanced in terms of the number of hand and foot techniques.

Composition 2: Power

- Favours strong powerful blocks and strikes.
- Favours weak or softer blocks and strikes.
- Balanced in terms of the number of techniques that use strong and weak force.

Composition 3: Speed

- Favours fast movements of the hands and feet.
- Favours slow actions.
- Balanced in terms of the number of techniques that use fast and slow actions.

Further explanation relating to the composition of patterns is discussed in the coloured belt pattern philosophy.

Taegeuk patterns
Philosophy

The first stage of the practitioner's development begins with learning 8 coloured belt patterns. The second stage consists of learning 9 black belt patterns. All patterns incorporate defensive and offensive actions. Blocking, kicking, striking and punching techniques are demonstrated on both sides of the body. This helps to develop or shape the body equally on the left and right sides. Taegeuk patterns consist of 18 to 27 movements and progress technically in terms of difficulty and complexity. Practitioners should keep in mind the philosophy that is attached to each pattern during performances.

The coloured belt patterns start with the practitioner standing in a ready stance. The feet are positioned shoulder width apart, and parallel with each other. Both fists are placed in front of the lower abdomen and one fist distance away from the body. There must be a gap of one fist in between the two fists; the fists are not touching. Importance of the ready stance must be emphasised, as it is the first and last movement of a pattern. Performing a pattern by count, step 1 is executed from the ready stance. Practitioners must be prepared mentally, thinking about what they are about to do in the ready stance, and apply oneself to the exercise from the beginning until the end. Performances must be spiritually strong enough to be beyond any distractions. On completion of the pattern, practitioners return to the same starting position in the ready stance. The pattern finishes when the ready stance has been completed and not, for example, step 18 of pattern 1, which by count is the last technique.

Figure 9.1   Ready stance

Taegeuk Pattern 1

Pattern 1 consists of basic techniques which are relatively easy to demonstrate. This routine is the foundation from which all the other forms are built, the beginning. The pattern represents 'heaven and light', symbolising the beginning of life, the source of creation. In order to sustain life, all living things need water (rain from the heavens) and light (the sun shines the light). This pattern comprises hand techniques with the fist clenched tight. Low, middle and high section blocks and middle section punches should be executed with force. Walking stances are mostly used throughout the pattern, assisting fast movements in the direction of travel. Leg techniques are minimal; a front kick is used two times in this routine.

Taegeuk Pattern 2

Pattern 2 represents 'joyfulness', symbolised by a lake. This pattern must be demonstrated in a relaxed, confident manner, representing strength of mind, which is characterised by the gentle but powerful nature of a lake. Hand and leg techniques are similar to pattern 1, although the front kick is performed more often. This pattern is the only coloured belt routine that contains a high section punch. Middle section punches are generally used throughout most patterns. The pace of the pattern is slow, as the forward stance is used more often. Practitioners must complete the forward stance so that they feel settled and balanced with both feet firmly on the ground before turning or moving on to the next step. The hand techniques must be performed with strong force.

Taegeuk Pattern 3

Pattern 3 represents 'fire and sun'. This routine features more combinations of kicking and punching techniques compared with patterns 1 and 2. The actions must be demonstrated with speed and enthusiasm, characteristic of sudden bursts of flickering fire. The fighting spirit of Taekwondo practitioners is encouraged by demonstrating this routine, which demands energy and passion. Techniques with a clenched fist must be performed with force. Open-hand techniques such as the knife-hand block and knife-hand strike are weaker or softer actions. The movements from one stance to the next are slower, due to the use of the forward stance, although speed is crucial when executing a combination of technique; for instance, step 2 - front kick followed by two middle section punches - must be executed continuously without pausing and with strong force.

Taegeuk Pattern 4

This pattern symbolises 'thunder and lightning'. This pattern is taught at 5th Kup level, which is seen as an advanced stage. The techniques within pattern 4 reflect a change in expectations and are technically more complex. Pattern 4 favours open-hand motions. Patterns 1, 2 and 3 mainly favour hand techniques with a clenched fist. Techniques at this advanced level are used more in free sparring, such as knife-hand blocks and side kicks. Free sparring can be dangerous and instil fear and panic. Practitioners must remain calm and act bravely in the presence of adversity, knowing that danger will soon pass, just like a thunderstorm leaving blue skies and sunshine. This pattern comprises hand and foot techniques that are executed with strong and weak force. The beginning of the pattern favours weaker open-hand techniques; these are strengthened with the assisted-hand, such as knife-hand guarding block and a combined downward palm block with a vertical spear-hand strike. The last 6 steps of the pattern favour strikes executed with force, inner blocks and middle section punches. Overall, the movements are slow, as the practitioner must pay attention to accuracy and balance, particularly in the back stance, when a front kick and inner block are performed at the same spot.

Taegeuk Pattern 5

Pattern 5 represents the 'wind'. The weather is gentle in nature, but it can be very strong and destructive. The techniques within this pattern, such as back-fist and elbow strikes, are executed within close proximity of an opponent. The actions must be performed with a strong, solid, aggressive approach, brushing away any resistance and penetrating an opponent's defence. The actions characterise gusts of wind: defences are blown away in sudden powerful bursts. Actions in this pattern favour hand and foot techniques which must be executed with a strong mind, using force. Forward stances slow down the pace of the pattern but provide stability and assist in the strength of techniques; for instance, steps 15 and 17, high section blocks, the motion is reinforced with the waist or body placed behind the technique.

Taegeuk Pattern 6

Pattern 6 represents 'water'. Water in its natural state is a liquid that is without form. Water is persistent, always flowing downstream and overcoming any obstacles in its path. Taekwondo practitioners must demonstrate this pattern with an awareness of versatility, persistence and patience, characteristic of moving water. This pattern favours kicking skills, which are used more than any other Kup grade form. The blocking actions are weaker but rely on footwork, encouraging the practitioner to pivot and turn, and move backwards, and avoid attacking techniques. The pattern relies on flexibility and agility for speed, which assist in generating powerful techniques. The concept of developing spiritual strength through controlled respiration is introduced in this routine. Step 10, twin low-section block, must be performed in slow motion with force and tensing the muscles. Breathing must be controlled so that on preparation of the technique the practitioner inhales through the nose and exhales slowly through the mouth on execution of the technique.

Taegeuk Pattern 7

Pattern 7 represents the strength and stability associated with a 'mountain'. Movements in this routine must be executed swiftly and stopping suddenly without losing balance. This represents decision-making on knowing when to stop and when to proceed without acting hastily. Solid, strong techniques executed in a forward stance help to produce power and accuracy. This pattern combines weaker open-hand techniques with strong closed-fist hand motions. Sequenced movements allow for slow and fast actions. Long forward stances provide a solid base to execute strong techniques while maintaining balance. Shorter stances such as the 'tiger', 'cross-legged' and 'side-horse riding' stances provide swift motions but can lack stability. Spiritual strength is developed in this pattern; the action follows a different approach to that of pattern 6. The wrapped fist (step 7) must be delivered with a softer motion with the muscles in the body relaxed, as opposed to tensing and using force. Breathing control is applied in the same way, inhaling through the nose on preparation of the technique and exhaling through the mouth on execution of the technique.

Taegeuk Pattern 8

Pattern 8 symbolises the 'earth'. This form reminds us to respect all forms of life. The earth is moist and heavy; it absorbs and nurtures everything. Living things grow and reach up towards the heavens. In death all things return to the earth. Earth is more powerful than any living thing and demands respect. Collectively, the coloured belt patterns provide the practitioner with an understanding of the basic techniques within Taekwondo. In one sense, the practitioner's journey or formal training has come to an end; however, the black belt patterns have yet to be learnt. The practitioner has come full circle and is preparing to continue training with a black belt tied around the waist. Familiar techniques are helpful to the new black belt; they help orientate and provide confidence to the practitioner embarking on a new journey as a black belt. The 'already known' helps support the individual as new techniques are introduced.

The beginning of learning

Pattern 8 and the 1st black belt pattern, Koryo, contain actions that are both simple and complex. With the foundations in place (the coloured belt patterns learnt), the practitioner is at the right place to begin learning advanced techniques. The two patterns are intertwined in the sense that practitioners must be persistent, patient and work hard in order to demonstrate either pattern to a good standard. The transition from a coloured belt to an established black belt is a critical stage of training. This is the last time that practitioners change the colour of their belt. Other similarities exist between pattern 8 and the black belt patterns. Two kihaps (a yell or sound made simultaneously with the execution of a technique) or more are used within the high grade patterns. Taegeuk forms 1 to 7 employ one kihap. Pattern 8 encourages controlled breathing at steps 6 and 8; this action (uppercut punch) must be executed with force by tensing the muscles. Dan grade patterns, with the exception of Taebaek and Chonkwon, incorporate numerous actions that are performed with controlled breathing. This assists in the development of spiritual or inner strength. Pattern 8 favours the use of hand techniques which are both weaker (open hand) and strong (clenched fist). Kicking techniques are kept to a minimum, although two movements, step 3 and step 19, are jumping kicks which have been introduced for the first time in the Taegeuk pattern series. Pattern 8 comprises movements that are fast and slow. Techniques performed in forward and tiger stances demand patience, accuracy and balance. Actions that are demonstrated in a back stance are sharper and faster.

Commitment, effort and spirit that Taekwondo practitioners demonstrate are rewarded with promotion through the two-stage grading system. The attainment of coloured belts and black belts is a highly praised and respected personal achievement. Having an understanding of the philosophy and disciplines that are interwoven within the patterns can lead to harmonisation of the body and mind. Taegeuk patterns assist in the development of physical strength - the body. Black belt patterns assist in the development of inner strength - the mind. Over time, by practising both sets of patterns, physical strength and mental strength expand. Ultimately, the individual's quality of life is enhanced.

Kihap

Taegeuk and Dan grade poomsae incorporate a 'breathing action' that is forced upward and outward from the diaphragm and assists in concentrating the mind while executing a technique. A 'kihap' or 'yell' can be described as a short exhalation of breath accompanied with a shout from the diaphragm and not the throat. The kihap unites the spirit and body, strengthening and enhancing the power in techniques. Controlled breathing, focused intent and physical co-ordination are aligned simultaneously with the execution of a technique; for example, a punch or kick. When a kihap is performed correctly, abdominal muscles tighten, forcing air out from the centre of the body, generating energy empowering the technique. A good focused kihap can be used to:
- Prepare the mind and body for the task that one is about to

undertake; in a sense a kind of 'wake-up call'.
- Intimidate an opponent, causing momentary hesitation or even making them move backwards or stumble and fall to the ground.
- Protect the body against strikes, tensing the muscles provides a solid shield and allows air to escape.
- Assist breath control to increase strength in special actions such as breaking techniques. This usually incorporates kicking or striking wooden boards (approximately 1 inch thick) as a test of skill and power.

Actions

Practitioners must aim to demonstrate patterns with correct, powerful techniques. Blocking, kicking and striking skills are demonstrated in thin air against an imaginary opponent of the same stature. This is important as the kicks and punches must be aimed at specific targets.

- High section target – face (philtrum).
- Middle section target – trunk (solar plexus).
- Low section target – abdomen (lower part of abdomen).

Under examination conditions - for instance, promotion tests or pattern competitions - competitors are judged on the control and accuracy of techniques. These are based on appropriate targets for individual performers. Practitioners executing a middle section punch that is delivered above their own solar plexus will be judged to have little control or understanding of what is perceived to be a correct middle section punch. Practitioners cannot claim that their imaginary opponent is taller than themselves, making the target higher. Basic techniques within patterns must be demonstrated as if the imaginary 'opponent' shares the same physique as the performer.

Patterns always start with blocking motions, serving to protect from an opponent's attack. This highlights the defensive nature and spirit of Taekwondo, promoting friendship, co-operation and the cultivation of harmony of the self and social environment. Blocking actions delivered with an appropriate level of power and force can be so damaging that they incapacitate an opponent's arms and legs. This can lead to the end of a confrontation without launching any attacking techniques. This suggests that the values of Taekwondo are of a generous nature, rather than acting in a socially unacceptable aggressive manner by initiating an attack. However, offensive motions, striking, punching or kicking may be necessary to overcome an aggressor for protection.

Centre point of gravity

Techniques need a solid base from which to launch defensive and offensive actions. Balance is a crucial factor that assists in power, accuracy and effectiveness of techniques. The core or centre of the body must be in a vertical position to maintain balance. Power comes from the lower abdomen, the centre point of gravity in the body; this is half way between the sides and half way between the front and back of the body. The hands and feet make physical contact with an opponent. Without an understanding of how to apply the body in terms of power, full impact potential can never be achieved. Stances in patterns influence the position of the body, which constantly change and move from one step to the next step. An awareness of the centre of gravity in relation to the position of the feet will help to achieve and maintain balance. The core must be kept vertical and above the midpoint between the feet.

Figure 9.2 Taegeuk patterns, stances and defensive actions

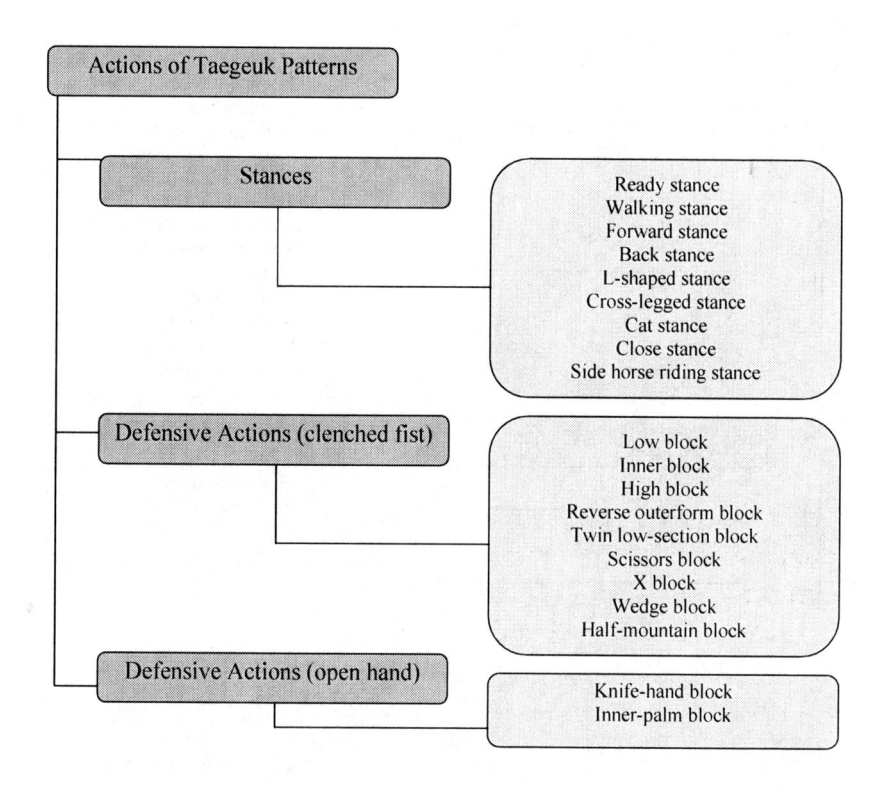

- **Actions of Taegeuk Patterns**
  - **Stances**
    - Ready stance
    - Walking stance
    - Forward stance
    - Back stance
    - L-shaped stance
    - Cross-legged stance
    - Cat stance
    - Close stance
    - Side horse riding stance
  - **Defensive Actions (clenched fist)**
    - Low block
    - Inner block
    - High block
    - Reverse outerform block
    - Twin low-section block
    - Scissors block
    - X block
    - Wedge block
    - Half-mountain block
  - **Defensive Actions (open hand)**
    - Knife-hand block
    - Inner-palm block

Figure 9.3 Taegeuk Patterns, offensive, kicking and assisted actions

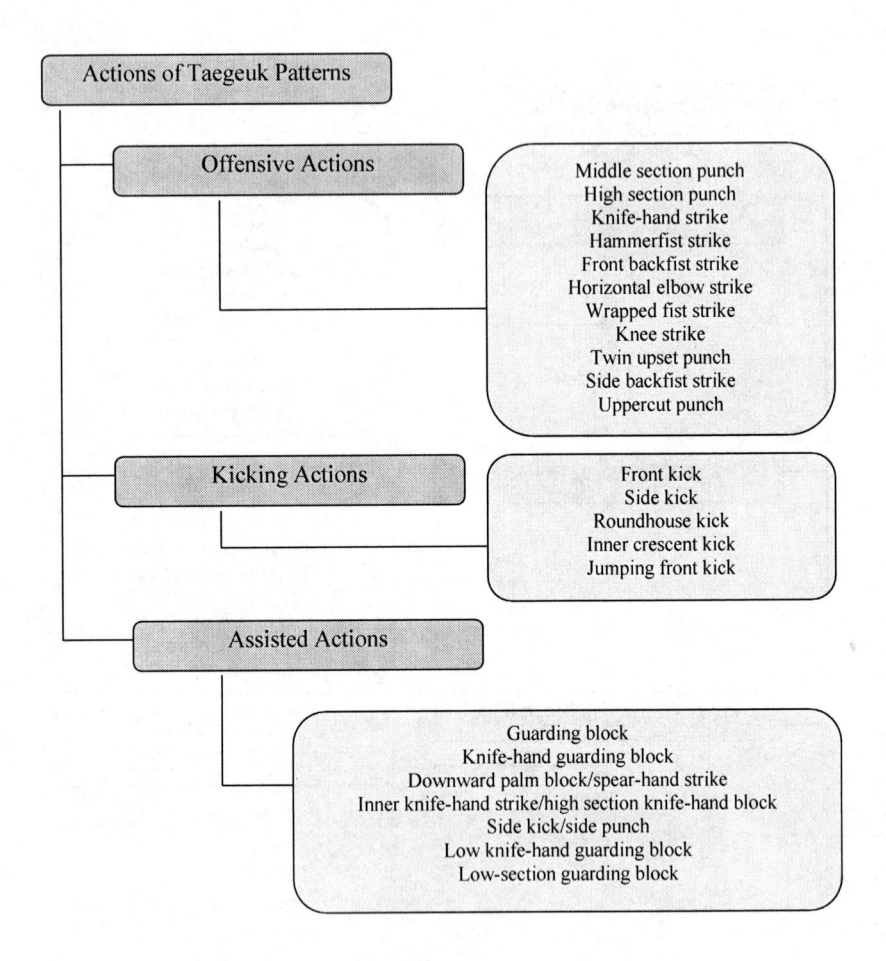

Actions of Taegeuk Patterns

- **Offensive Actions**
  - Middle section punch
  - High section punch
  - Knife-hand strike
  - Hammerfist strike
  - Front backfist strike
  - Horizontal elbow strike
  - Wrapped fist strike
  - Knee strike
  - Twin upset punch
  - Side backfist strike
  - Uppercut punch

- **Kicking Actions**
  - Front kick
  - Side kick
  - Roundhouse kick
  - Inner crescent kick
  - Jumping front kick

- **Assisted Actions**
  - Guarding block
  - Knife-hand guarding block
  - Downward palm block/spear-hand strike
  - Inner knife-hand strike/high section knife-hand block
  - Side kick/side punch
  - Low knife-hand guarding block
  - Low-section guarding block

Transition from Kup grade to Dan grade

Taekwondo practitioners that have successfully passed a promotion test to black belt status must change their approach in the way they execute basic blocking actions. Over time, through repetitive demonstration of all of the Taegeuk poomsae, the development of physical strength is achievable. Practitioners will usually find that the basic action, such as the delivery of a middle section punch, become automatic and, to a degree, powerful. Dan grades must look at the level of power that they can deliver in a middle section punch and compare this to the level of power that they achieve in executing low section and inner blocks. Usually, the defensive blocking actions will be less powerful than the punching motion. At black belt level, enhanced power in delivery of a block is directly related to the practitioner's mindset. At this advanced stage of development, a new way of thinking should be emerging. The correct way of thinking about all techniques at this level includes calculating the correct levels of power needed and applying development to all the techniques learned at Kup grade level. Newly graded 1st Dan practitioners need to guard against complacency, making sure that they do not accept their pre-Dan standards of performance as acceptable. The level to which this has been understood by the holder of a new Dan grade will be revealed by the demonstration of their patterns. Actions must be delivered with the same mentality as when a punch is launched. Blocking actions, with the fist clenched, must be delivered with the idea of striking an opponent's arms or legs, inflicting damage to incapacitate the limbs. The contact area on the low and inner blocks is the same as the contact area of the clenched-hand used in a Hammerfist strike, the side of the fist next to the little finger. Practitioners must be consciously aware of the contact area when demonstrating patterns. Blocking actions become more focused and sharp, striking harder with real intent and purpose. In time, the same mentality can be applied to open-hand defensive techniques, although these actions are generally weaker at the wrist and it takes longer to develop power. Demonstrating patterns without mistakes at a Kup grade level is excellent. This is expected at a black belt level. Newly promoted Kup grades to 1st Dan black belt must realise that expectations increase. Individual practitioners are encouraged to show a higher degree of power, control and determination. The 'way' in Taekwondo, the spirit is further developed.

Figure 9.4
Low section block

Figure 9.5
Inner block

Figure 9.6
Hammerfist strike

Basic kicking action

Basic kicks that are mainly incorporated in the Taegeuk and Dan grade patterns are front, side, roundhouse and back kicks. It is important to have an understanding of the ideal shape or posture in preparation and execution of the techniques. An awareness of the position of the supporting foot, the foot on the ground, is crucial to obtain control and balance. The arms must be controlled so that they assist in the motion of a kicking action and so that a performance is tidy and neat. The arms must not be allowed to move around in the air with no real control or purpose.

Figure 9.7   Training Matrix: Basic Kicks

Action: Type of Kick	Preparation: Knee position with the leg bent	Execution: Supporting foot position	Execution: Arm position
Front kick	Raise the knee high in front.	45 degrees	Guarding block
Push kick	Raise the knee high up to the chest. Keep the upper body leaning forwards over the kick; do not lean backwards.	160 degrees	Guarding block
Raising kick	Raise the leg straight up; do not bend the knee. If the target is close, bend the knee to clear the target and kick with the leg straight.	90 degrees to 100 degrees	Guarding block
Side kick	Raise the knee and shin parallel to the floor, pull in tight to help deliver a powerful kick.	170 degrees to 180 degrees	In front of the chest

Back kick	After turning, raise the knee high in front of the chest. Similar to a front kick but pull the knee in close.	170 degrees to 180 degrees	In front of the chest
Roundhouse kick	Raise the knee high in front of the chest, similar to the front kick. On completion, the knee will be parallel to the floor, similar to a side kick position.	170 degrees to 180 degrees	In front of the chest or the leading hand can move down behind the back.

Training continues.

Chapter 10

Power

Developing power

Taekwondo practitioners must always look for ways to improve their own personal standard. This can be in terms of flexibility, fitness, speed and power. One of the main themes that is constantly being promoted by instructors is the development of power. The level or degree of power is observable in practical tasks such as patterns and breaking techniques. Both tasks require appropriate levels of power. Patterns consist of actions that must be performed with variations of slow, soft and strong force. Breaking techniques require practitioners to execute a hand or foot technique with just enough force to break, for example, wooden boards or plastic breakable boards. By adding more boards, e.g. two or three, more power is needed to successfully complete the task.

Power implies possession of physical and mental abilities or capacity to do something. Physical power includes the ability to exert enough force to drive or push an adversary away and control a confrontational situation. Physical, muscular strength must be equal to the momentum of an opponent's attack in order to effectively defend oneself. Mental strength includes the ability to withstand the pressure of an attack and possess the quality to deal with pain or stress. Practitioners must possess the power, strength and belief to overwhelm an opponent, influence and control a situation or behaviour of others, with supremacy. Defensive abilities must be used to induce an adversary to behave differently than they otherwise would. In order to protect oneself, the use of physical force to restrain or strike someone to cause physical harm is sometimes necessary. Practitioners must possess the energy, liveliness and power to work hard and concentrate on the task in hand. Regular, repetitive physical exercise, appropriate dietary intake and rest assist in the development of strength and power.

As practitioners progress through the grading system, they will be able to feel that their techniques are easier to deliver, faster, more powerful and effective. Techniques become stronger as the practitioner matures in ability and status. There are many aspects to a technique which need consideration if a practitioner intends to enhance power. Power is discussed with reference to a middle section punch, which is the most frequently used technique in patterns: approximately 119 times. A middle section punch is usually prepared with the fist clenched tight at the side of the waist, with the palm-side facing up. This can more easily be practised in a horse-riding stance or forward stance. The main principles include: tensing the muscles, using a twisting motion, speed control, use of reaction hand, eye control, breathing control and spirit.

1. At the point of impact, at the last possible moment, the fist must be tensed so that the punch is rigid and strong. Tensing the muscles assists in controlling the motion and lessens the risk of injury to the practitioner.
2. Simultaneously, at the moment of impact the fist must twist (and tense) in a snapping action so that the palm of the fist is facing down. This twisting motion brings power to the punch.
3. A punch must be delivered with speed, accelerating towards the end of the technique, creating a sharp, fast action.

Techniques that are too slow, hesitant or apprehensive will lack power.

4. At the same time as executing a middle section punch, the opposite hand or reaction hand is pulled back to the side of the waist. This counter-balances the movement and increases the force of the punch. The body is bilateral and essentially symmetrical. When a technique is launched, the body compensates the action with a reaction. It is practically impossible to stop the left shoulder moving backwards when a punch is thrown with the right fist, moving the right shoulder forwards. Once a force is exerted, it exerts a force back in the opposite direction, equal in magnitude to the initial force. This principle applies to physical systems and is acknowledged in Newton's third law of motion: 'To every action there is an equal and opposite reaction.'

5. Eye control refers to focus, accuracy and precise contact areas of the clenched fist and of the intended target. Practitioners must turn the head and look in the direction of travel, focusing on striking the solar plexus. An approximate strike towards the middle section of the body or chest of an adversary would not be as effective. Techniques that are delivered away from the centre line of the body are easier to block or avoid. The striking points of the fist are the large knuckles of the second and third fingers. Eye control is crucial in delivering a focused damaging strike as opposed to a technique that is loosely executed with no real purpose or direction.

6. Breathing control assists in creating a natural, unforced and powerful technique. The breath must be inhaled on preparation of each technique and exhaled with the punching action. On contact, at the last moment, the remainder of the breath is exhaled. This ensures that the technique is delivered with the body in a relaxed state. Tensing the muscles too soon inhibits the speed of a technique and wastes energy.

7. Spirit refers to the way in which practitioners train. Regular training with a positive attitude, hard work and determination enhances physical and mental strength. The body and mind

must be used as a single unit, with an awareness of the principles that are associated with the development of power. This assists in the ability to exert considerable force in offensive and defensive actions.

Power involves the ability to manipulate and control a situation and possess the skills to exert force to incapacitate an adversary. The points discussed should not be looked at as individual aspects that can enhance power, but as factors that are interwoven. With an awareness of these principles collectively working together, performances will be stronger, more powerful and more effective. Practitioners, over time, will feel the difference. Onlookers will be able to see the difference. This is noticeable as practitioners mature, gain experience and progress through the Kup grade and Dan grade curriculum.

Strength and power

Patterns are essentially exercises that assist in the development of physical strength and power. How a pattern is performed provides incite into a practitioner's strengths and weaknesses. Performances can reveal areas where practitioners lack power, balance and flexibility. Generally, power is more noticeable in middle section punches and weaker in most blocking actions. Practitioners must work hard to increase their abilities in many areas to produce a performance of a pattern to a high standard.

Figure 10.1   Development of strength and power

Physical Actions	Promotes
1. Blocks, strikes and kicks.	Improves accuracy, speed and power.

2. Moving from one stance to the next stance. — Strengthens the muscles in the legs.
3. Combinations of techniques. — Improves co-ordination, agility and speed.
4. Symmetry, movements repeated both sides of the body. — Develops the left and right side of the body, equally; shape and strength.

Mental Actions	Promotes
1. Mental attention.	Improves concentration and focus.
2. Breathing control.	Improves cardiovascular fitness and inner strength.
3. Repetition and perseverance.	Furthers understanding of patience.

In The Main	Promotes
1. In a practical sense.	Learn self-defence system.
2. Patterns.	Education, health and fun.
3. Exercise (patterns).	Enhances strength, fitness and co-ordination.
4. Experience.	Decreases mistakes, promotes confidence and composure.
5. Flexibility, strength and fitness.	Assists in performances at a higher level or standard.
6. Personal development.	Achieves promotion and personal goals.

Final Thought	Promotes
1. By practising patterns.	The true nature and spirit of Taekwondo are discovered.

Training continues.

Chapter 11

Breaking techniques

Breaking techniques

Martial art skills that involve breaking wooden boards, roof tiles, house bricks and breeze blocks are normally used in promotion tests, demonstrations or competitions. These materials have now largely been superseded by plastic breakable boards, plastic roof tiles and plastic house bricks which can be pushed back together and reused. This type of equipment has a huge advantage over natural raw materials due to the expense, availability and disposal of the destroyed products. Practitioners should aim to gain experience and test their technical skills and power on both the wooden boards and plastic breakable boards. The materials behave differently when successfully broken and in a failed attempt. Safety is an important factor for the practitioner attempting a breaking task and for assistants who are holding or supporting the board about to be broken. Boards, on being struck, can fly into the air out of control, and fall on to unprotected feet. Experienced instructors should always be present during such tasks. Usually, practitioners under the age of 16 are not permitted to break boards in promotion tests.

Material

Wooden boards used for promotion tests are normally soft pine. The grain is straight, easily perceived and will break with relative ease along the grain. Avoid hard woods such as mahogany or oak. Boards are usually cut 10 inches wide, 12 inches long and three-quarters of an inch thick. The width runs parallel with the grain and the length is cut across or perpendicular to the grain.

Speed and accuracy

A demonstration of power is the result of techniques that are executed with accuracy and speed. Actions that are very fast but miss the target due to lack of control are ineffectual and can be dangerous to the practitioner and assistants. Diminished speed could be the result of practitioners hesitating in attempting to break boards for fear of the risk of injury or pain. Successful breaking techniques do not bring about any pain. Bare hands or feet on striking a board with high velocity do not have time to deform, get squashed and produce pain, but rather penetrate straight through the material. Power breaks can be described as a test where a board that is about to be broken is supported, so that it can not move. In speed breaks, boards are held lightly between two fingers and can easily move with a kicking or punching technique. Speed and accuracy are crucial for both tasks, although speed is more of a critical factor in speed breaking. The strength of an individual is meaningless if a board is not struck with sufficient accuracy and velocity.

Expectations

Practitioners must always aim to improve and perfect their techniques to the best of their ability. Breaking techniques must be executed with precise placement of the hand or foot to achieve success. Practitioners can fail a promotion test if they do not manage to complete a breaking task. This is especially important at the higher Dan grade status, where expectations are very high. Master grades should aim to successfully complete breaking tasks ten times out of ten attempts.

Distance

Judging the distance between oneself and the target is an important part of the process for a breaking technique. Practitioners must 'measure up' once or twice if necessary by placing, for example, the foot against the centre of the board. Pinpoint accuracy must be achieved. Ideally, a technique needs to penetrate and go beyond a board by three to four inches. Strikes that are too far away and only just touch the surface of a board use up power before actual contact. This results in little or no power left to penetrate the target. Strikes that are too close act like a pushing motion; this may still break the board or the practitioner may bounce off the target. There is not enough space or distance in which to fully extend the leg and generate sufficient speed and power. Heavy equipment such as a punch bag is ideal for the development of power.

Concentration

Mental concentration enhances physical power. The mind must be applied with focused concentration and the body relaxed so that all the force of a blow is directed at a specific point in space. The mind must be focused 100 per cent on the task in hand. Other thoughts or distractions draw on energy and lessen the power of techniques. Physical strength by itself is not always enough to break boards. A naturally very strong person may not be able to successfully break boards without focusing their power properly. Practitioners must be in complete control of themselves and the activity. The kihap is usually performed twice by practitioners during a breaking task. The first kihap lets the assistants (who are holding the board) know that it is about to be struck. This helps to ensure the board is held firm. The first kihap also assists the practitioner who is about to break the board to concentrate their power on the task in hand. The second kihap is applied with the strike, on impact of the target, to assist in generating force.

Breathing

The main principles of power include breathing control and tensing the muscles. The body must be in a relaxed state before the blow is struck, breathing out and tensing the muscles on impact. This is accompanied with a kihap which assists in tensing the muscles and exhaling the last remaining breath.

Assistants

Assistants who are holding boards that are about to be struck play a crucial role. The boards must not be allowed to move, otherwise the exercise may result in failure. They must be held firm so that the power will go 100 per cent into the target, instead of moving back in the same direction as the strike. Assistants must place the heel of the palm against the back of the board with their fingers curled over the top and underneath. The fingers will be on the same side of the board that is going to be struck. The arms must be rigid so that the board will not move when the blow lands. It is up to the practitioner who is about to attempt a breaking technique to position the angle of the board according to the type of technique used and ensure that the grain of the wood is running in the appropriate direction. Practitioners must take control of the situation and not rely on assistants or other parties to set the scene. Practitioners must be happy with the situation before they attempt to break the board.

Confidence

To ensure that confidence remains intact, the principles of breaking techniques must be fully understood. Techniques must be practised so that they can be executed with accuracy, speed and power. Practitioners must be able to transmit the force of a blow through a board without diminished power. Techniques must become habitual so that they can be delivered at an unconscious level. This assists in generating techniques with incredible speed and in breaking boards cleanly, with no pain. Attempting techniques that are beyond the capabilities of individuals will only serve to destroy their confidence. Practice is essential. The more one puts in, the more one gets out.

Figure 11.1   Self-Confidence

(a) Preparation

(b) Unprepared

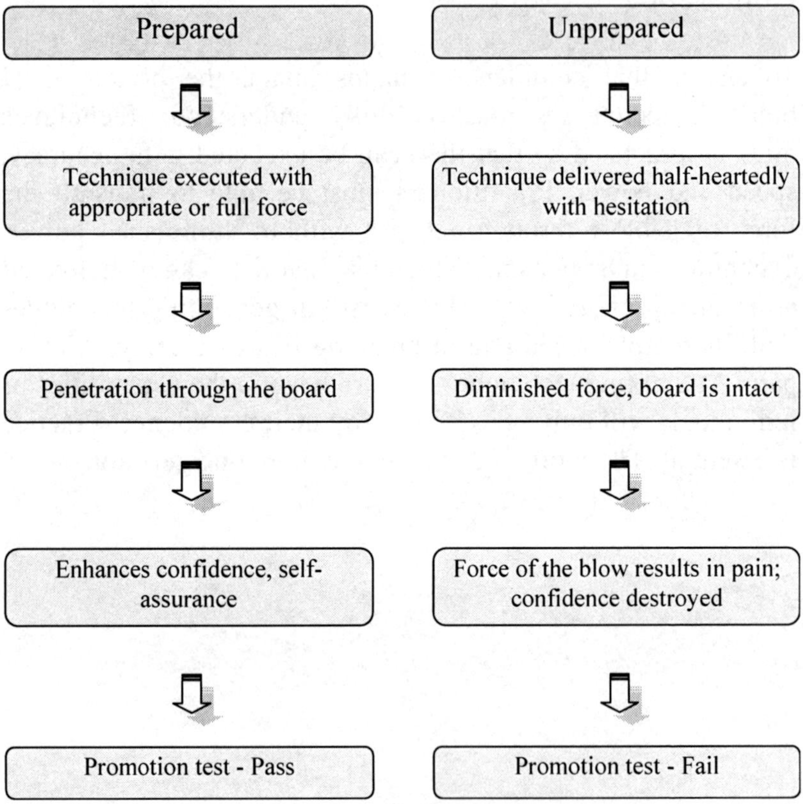

Prepared	Unprepared
⬇	⬇
Technique executed with appropriate or full force	Technique delivered half-heartedly with hesitation
⬇	⬇
Penetration through the board	Diminished force, board is intact
⬇	⬇
Enhances confidence, self-assurance	Force of the blow results in pain; confidence destroyed
⬇	⬇
Promotion test - Pass	Promotion test - Fail

Perfection

Education of Taekwondo involves learning and understanding the principles and techniques of the martial art system. Regular training regimes become part of a practitioner's way of life. Physical and mental strength is enhanced through activities based on the concept of change and movement. Personal goals and achievements are accomplished over months and years of practice. Perfection is thought to be achieved when hand and foot techniques are demonstrated flawlessly with precision and power. Practitioners must always aim to reach the highest standard possible. There is always room for improvement, as techniques can be executed a little more smoothly and with more power. In this sense, perfection can never be achieved. In pursuit of perfection, Taekwondo practitioners discover the values, spirit and true nature of the martial art.

Figure 11.2   Education and perfection

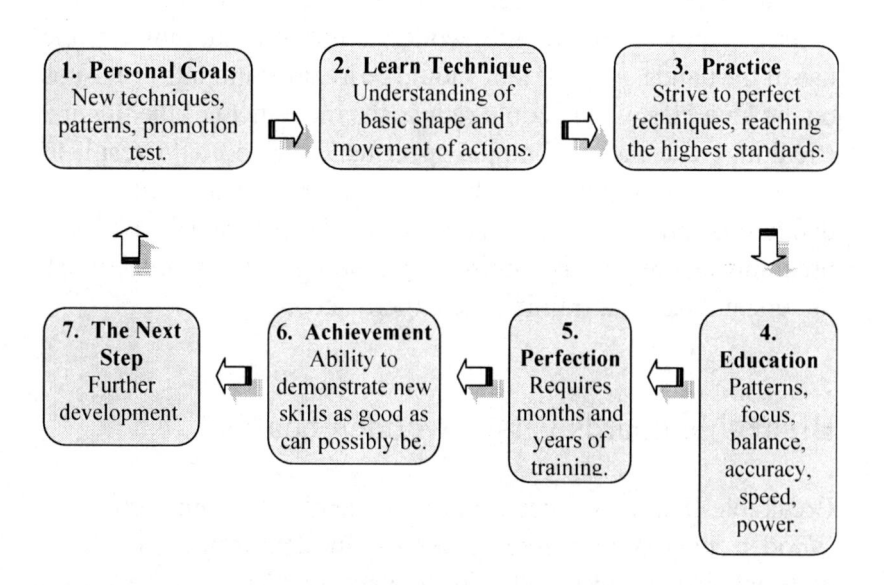

1. **Personal Goals** — New techniques, patterns, promotion test.
2. **Learn Technique** — Understanding of basic shape and movement of actions.
3. **Practice** — Strive to perfect techniques, reaching the highest standards.
4. **Education** — Patterns, focus, balance, accuracy, speed, power.
5. **Perfection** — Requires months and years of training.
6. **Achievement** — Ability to demonstrate new skills as good as can possibly be.
7. **The Next Step** — Further development.

Box 1. Setting personal goals is a never-ending process.
Box 5. Perfection is never really achieved.
Box 6. Achievement relates to the development of physical and mental abilities.

Conditioning

Basic breaking techniques with the feet include a front kick, side kick, roundhouse kick (with the ball of the foot), back kick and back hook kick. Breaking techniques with the hand include a knife-hand strike, ridge-hand strike, palm-heel strike, middle section punch and horizontal elbow strike. These actions rely on the product 'accuracy' and 'speed' which produce 'power'. The idea of conditioning the hands and feet to the extent that hard skin and calluses are formed is unnecessary. Considering that caring for the body, harmonisation of the mind and body, are central concepts of Taekwondo, this type of approach seems to be superfluous. Practitioners should not carry out any exercise if they are not entirely happy. Everyday life, work, studies or leisure involve the use of the hands. Actions that should be avoided include press-ups on the knuckles, which could reduce the movement of the fingers. Breaking with the finger tips, spear-hand strike could result in broken or distorted fingers. Breaking with the head is potentially dangerous and may result in concussion. Risk of injury with basic breaking techniques is minimal, providing correct procedures, understandings and training are experienced.

Breakable boards versus wooden boards

Breakable boards are used more frequently in promotion tests. Wooden boards are used generally in demonstrations. Both materials behave differently in the way they break and draw on different technical skills. Plastic breakable boards will only break in one place along the centre line. Breakable boards require the same amount of power to break every time as they are simply pushed back together and reused. The dynamics of a board do not change. Once the degree of power has been identified, accuracy becomes the crucial factor in successfully breaking the plastic board. Wooden boards can break in several places, top middle or bottom, anywhere in fact along the grain. This leaves room for error as regards pinpoint accuracy. Wood varies in strength or resistance due to the level of moisture in the material and variations in the grain running through the board. The straighter and closer together the grain, the easier it is to break the boards. This suggests that power is the critical element as opposed to accuracy. Wood is softer to the touch and makes a nice sound when it breaks.

Assistants who are holding material about to be broken could sustain injury if the correct procedures and level of caution are not adhered to. Wood and plastic boards behave slightly differently when they are struck. Common mistakes include techniques that are inaccurate and delivered with too much force. Breakable boards, when they are struck with excessive power and do not hit the centre line, do not break. The force of the blow is absorbed by the assistant holding the board and the practitioner and could be painful for both. Even when the board breaks, excessive force could send the two halves flying out of control into the air, as they are too difficult to keep hold of. This could easily hit someone in the face, eye or land on someone's foot. Assistants holding the board about to be struck must wear safety glasses and training shoes for protection. Too much power and a lack of accuracy with techniques on wooden boards are often more forgiving. Boards can break when a blow lands off-centre along the grain.

Figure 11.3   Breakable boards versus wooden boards

Breakable Board	Wooden Board
• Primarily a test of accuracy. • Will only break in the centre of the board. • Power is a secondary factor. • Resistance of the board is fixed. • Good tool for practicing techniques and for building confidence. • Assistants who are holding the board are more at risk to injury if a technique is executed with too much power and is inaccurate.	• Primarily a test of power. • Will break virtually anywhere along the grain of the board. • Accuracy is a secondary factor. • Resistance of boards varies. • Confidence can be knocked back if practitioners fail to break the board. • Assistants who are holding the board are less likely to be injured if a technique is executed with too much power and is inaccurate.

Breaking techniques on wooden and breakable boards: procedure

1. Position the height of the board to suit the stature of the practitioner and according to the type of technique used to break the board.
2. Position the angle of the board so that the breaking technique impacts at an angle of 90 degrees to the target. For example, for front kicks the board is angled at 45 degrees with the ground. For side, back and turning kicks the board must be held vertically.
3. Check that the grain or centre line of the breakable board is running in the appropriate direction according to the type of breaking technique. For example, for front, side and back

kicks the grain must run parallel with the ground.
4. Practitioners must stand at an appropriate distance from the target and assume a guarding stance.
5. Practitioners can measure up once or twice if necessary to check distance.
6. Eye control: practitioners must look at the board with focused concentration, keeping in mind the task in hand.
7. Practitioners must kihap to inform the assistants who are holding the board that they are about to strike the target. This also acts in assisting the practitioner to focus their mind on the task in hand.
8. Practitioners must kihap a second time when the board is struck, on impact. If successful and the board breaks, confidence remains intact and enhanced. OR, if unsuccessful and the board has not broken, this could result in damaging the confidence of the practitioner. Confidence that has been damaged could take a long time to repair.
9. Practitioners must return to a guarding stance after the board has been struck.
10. Eye control: practitioners must continue to look at the board even after breaking the board, and assume a guarding stance. This assists with focused concentration and eliminates a possible lapse in concentration and failure.

The whole procedure should be completed in approximately 2 minutes. This includes setting the scene and breaking the board for basic hand and leg techniques. Multiple breaks take slightly longer.

Practising breaking techniques using breakable boards: procedure

1. Position the breakable board to the required height.
2. Check the angle of the board.
3. Check the board is the correct way up in regards to the centre line.

4. Stand at an appropriate distance from the board in a guarding stance.
5. Eye control: practitioners must focus concentration on the task in hand.
6. Instructors must emphasise that the aim of the exercise at this point is not to break the board but to pay close attention to the control and accuracy of the technique.
7. Instructors must encourage practitioners to measure up several times, checking control and balance, pinpoint accuracy, tensing the muscles on contact with the board and that appropriate parts of the body are striking the surface of the board.
8. Every time practitioners measure up they should be encouraged to gradually increase the speed of every kick or strike. With every action, practitioners must remain focused, analysing accuracy and proficiency, making minor adjustments to the technique if necessary.
9. In time, the board will break as the speed of the technique gradually increases. This provides the practitioner with the knowledge of how much power is needed to break the board. If the board does not break after approximately 6 to 8 attempts, inform the practitioner that they can try again later and remind them that the idea was not to break the board. This provides practitioners with the opportunity to try breaking techniques without the pressure of having to break the board. Failure otherwise could destroy one's self-confidence.
10. Return to guarding stance at the end of every practice kick or strike.

Training continues.

Chapter 12

Dan grade promotion

Grading

Promotion within Taekwondo involves practitioners demonstrating an array of techniques in front of a panel of examiners. This includes patterns, sparring, self-defence and breaking techniques. Grades are an indication of the length of time practitioners have trained and are linked to levels of understanding and knowledge. This is guided by obligatory time periods and minimum age requirements paired with promotion tests. Patterns form a major part of examinations, which assist in revealing the practitioner's physical and mental strengths and weaknesses. Levels of fitness, flexibility, co-ordination and concentration are assessed by examiners. Practitioners must demonstrate kicking and punching skills with accuracy, control and power to certain pre-determined levels in order to attain the next grade. Performances must include behaviour that demonstrates the principles and values that underpin Taekwondo. The 'way' or 'spirit' of Taekwondo includes attitudes of self-discipline, self-control, determination and indomitable spirit. Courtesy, respect and politeness are expected at all times.

Table 12.1 Patterns and minimum time and age limits required for Dan Grade promotion tests.

Dan Grade to be promoted	Compulsory Pattern	Appointed Pattern	Minimum time required	Minimum age required
1st Kup to 1st Dan	Taegeuk 8	Taegeuk 1-7	6 months	–
1st Dan to 2nd Dan	Koryo	Taegeuk 1-8	1 year	–
2nd Dan to 3rd Dan	Keumgang	Taegeuk 1-8 and Koryo	2 years	–
3rd Dan to 4th Dan	Taebaek	Taegeuk 1-8, Koryo and Keumgang	3 years	21 years and above
4th Dan to 5th Dan	Pyongwon and Sipjin	Koryo, Keumgang and Taebaek	4 years	25 years and above
5th Dan to 6th Dan	Sipjin and Jitae	Taebaek and Pyongwon	5 years	30 years and above
6th Dan to 7th Dan	Chonkwon	Pyongwon, Sipjin and Jitae	6 years	36 years and above
7th Dan to 8th Dan	Hansu	Sipjin, Jitae and Chonkwon	8 years	44 years and above

| 8th Dan to 9th Dan | Ilyeo | Jitae, Chonkwon and Hansu | 9 years | 53 years and above |
| 9th Dan to 10th Dan | Theory (No pattern) | Decided by Technical Committee | Decided by Technical Committee | 60 years and above |

Dan Grading Syllabus

Practitioners must obtain approval from their Instructor in order to undertake the Dan grading test.

1. Pattern compulsory.

Practitioners must demonstrate one or more compulsory pattern(s) according to their grade (see Table 12.1).

2. Pattern practitioner's choice.

Practitioners must choose and demonstrate one of the appointed patterns according to their grade (see Table 12.1).

3. Pattern examiners choice.

Practitioners must demonstrate any of the appointed patterns chosen by examiners. Usually two patterns are selected which have not previously been demonstrated in the grading.

4. One-step pre-arranged sparring.

Pre-arranged fighting consists of two practitioners working together demonstrating defensive and offensive actions. One practitioner is assigned the role of the defender, while the other is the attacker. The attacker assumes a forward stance with a low section block (Figure 6.6). The defender, facing the attacker, assumes a ready stance (Figure 6.3). The attacker advances with a right hand middle section punch, unless the defender has otherwise requested a high or low section punch. The defender blocks or avoids the attack and executes a counter-attack. Alternating attacks with the right and left side are not required.

5.   Self-defence techniques.

Practitioners must assume a ready stance. The feet are shoulder-width apart, with the arms positioned naturally at the sides of the body. Practitioners must remain relaxed and in control of the situation. Actions are not as aggressive or so direct in the same way as pre-arranged sparring. Various attackers advance from any direction, front, side or behind, with grabbing and holding manoeuvres to the wrist, neck, shoulder, lapel, waist, hair and head. Practitioners must defend themselves by breaking free from the attacks. These actions can be followed up with appropriate counter-attacks.

6.   One-for-one sparring.

One-for-one fighting must be performed virtually on the spot with a partner and maintaining a safe distance, approximately 3 feet apart. This allows practitioners to use free expression and demonstrate a variety of explosive, fast kicking skills, without the pressure of being hit by counter-attacks. Offensive techniques and counter-attacks must be executed with appropriate targets in mind.

7. Free sparring.

Free fighting must be demonstrated with a partner with self-control. This includes controlling hand and leg techniques and decision-making of when and when not to launch attacks and counter-attacks to prevent injury. Light contact is permitted. The use of protective equipment such as body armour and head gear is at the discretion of the examiners.

8. Breaking techniques.

Breaking techniques are assessed on whether the board is successfully broken and that contact is made with the correct part of the foot, hand or arm. Practitioners must be prepared to execute a variety of foot or hand techniques, which is at the discretion of the examiners. Basic breaking techniques with the feet include front, side, turning, back and hook kicks. Basic breaking techniques with the hands include knife-hand, palm and elbow strikes. Practitioners under 16 years of age are not required to demonstrate breaking techniques.

9. Short discussion or interview.

Practitioners are asked questions by the examination panel concerning Taekwondo theory and philosophy that is appropriate to their current grade. Personal experiences, ambitions and goals concerning Taekwondo are also discussed.

10. Thesis (Practitioners testing for 4th Dan and above only).

Practitioners must submit a thesis concerning Taekwondo values and philosophy with emphasis on their personal experiences, achievements and ambitions. The thesis should be no less than 10 pages of A4 size (21cm x 30cm) paper.

Expectations

'Tae', to kick, and 'Kwon', to punch, are in one sense easier concepts to understand. 'Do', the way in Tae kwon do is the hardest part of the martial art to grasp or appreciate. The 'way' relates to a way of life or the journey of practitioners that encompasses the values, principles and disciplines underpinning Taekwondo. The 'way' or 'Do' can be expressed with one word, 'spirit', associated with the behaviour or way in which practitioners train. Concentration and determination are key attributes of the Taekwondo spirit and assist in personal development.

- Concentration ⇨ Eye control, focus ⇨ Mental stamina
- Determination ⇨ Achieve power ⇨ Physical stamina

A practitioner's abilities mature as they progress through the coloured belt and black belt grading system. Techniques develop pinpoint accuracy and power which leads to effective defensive and offensive actions. Higher technical standards combined with a serious approach or attitude are recognised and rewarded with promotion. Another type of reward is the emotional 'feel good' factor surrounding self-esteem and self-confidence on the attainment of personal goals. Practitioners are expected to develop an understanding of the way of Taekwondo, to show respect and commitment to their club and instructors. Practitioners must aim to:
- Establish a regular training routine. Attend classes with a high level of attendance and punctuality.

- Set personal goals, personal development, competitions and promotion.
- Apply oneself to training, work hard.
- Strive for perfection of techniques and exercises.
- Aim to develop a high overall standard with correct knowledge-based systems.
- Encourage and support other practitioners in their progress and development.
- Gain experience through competitions, seminars, grading and other activities.

Promotion

Taegeuk and Dan Grade patterns are practised throughout the world and are structured and promoted by the Kukkiwon, the World Headquarters of Taekwondo. This provides standardisation of Taekwondo techniques throughout the world. Performances are judged on eye control, spirit, focus, speed control, strength control, flexibility and balance. Through centuries of development and adaptation, Taekwondo examiners have gained excellent understandings of both the principles of Taekwondo and the processes involved in developing individual practitioners. Individual interpretation of patterns is welcomed if the techniques used adhere to Taekwondo principles.

Practitioners testing for 1st Dan black belt must demonstrate a basic understanding of how to perform patterns. Some power throughout the test must be evident. Testing for 2nd Dan, practitioners with more experience must be able to demonstrate sharper, more powerful techniques with a higher degree of control and concentration. 3rd Dan participants must exhibit a higher level of confidence, flair and enthusiasm. Performances must capture the spirit of Taekwondo. 4th Dan participants must be confident in their approach. Techniques must be executed with a higher degree of effectiveness, focused concentration, balance and composure. Participants testing for 5th

Dan must show composure, confidence and effectiveness in every area of their grading. Techniques must not be rushed. Performances must include a variety of techniques demonstrated with control and spirit. Respect and courtesy to other participants and examiners must be evident at all times. 6th Dan participants must perform to a very high standard, demonstrating power, balance, speed control, rhythm and timing. Patterns must be demonstrated with imagination, incorporating the characteristics and meanings that are inextricably interwoven with each routine. 7th Dan participants must show maturity in their approach and have a good understanding of the philosophy and principles of Taekwondo. 8th Dan is associated with that of a learned man and the understanding that training is a life-long learning process. 9th Dan is associated with oneness, harmonisation of the mind and body.

Discipline

- Patterns must be performed with power, control, accuracy and style. Actions must have the appearance of smooth, tidy transactions from one step to the next step. Thought must be applied to the preparation, transition and execution of every movement. To create a style that assists in creating beautiful, powerful actions, practitioners must perform with an awareness of the disciplines that underlie patterns.
- Finish techniques: Movements must finish with the hand and foot movement stopping simultaneously and completely before moving on to the next step. This assists powerful, committed actions with no additional or wasted movement.
- Breathing control: Controlled and correct breathing throughout routines enhances stamina, power and spirit. Practitioners should not have the appearance of gasping for breath during or at the end of the exercise.
- Reaction hand: The opposite hand must be used simultaneously with the execution of techniques. This action assists in the

presentation of controlled, tidy, disciplined movements and enhances power.
- Eye control: Assists in accuracy, speed and power. Practitioners that look in the direction of movement (not down to the floor) present a stronger and more confident performance.
- Hips: The core of the body or waist assists in generating power. Stances must be correct with correct posture and shape. The core must be kept in a vertical position.
- Guarding block: Front kicks are used more than any other leg technique within patterns. When a front kick is executed, the arms must be drawn in front of the body into a guarding position. This creates a tidy, controlled movement and prevents the arms from moving around freely with no real control or idea of where to place the arms.
- Naturally bending: The reaction arm must be used on preparation of techniques with the idea of placing the arm in front of the body, similar to a middle section punch. The arm is slightly bent and relaxed, with the fist lightly clenched. This creates a good, tidy style in pattern performances. With the arm outstretched and ready to pull back with the execution of a technique with the opposite hand, the action is natural, direct and fast. Ultimately, the practitioner in a sparring match, who is faster, will win.

Attention to detail

- Footwork: Most movements from one stance to another stance involve moving one foot and pivoting on the other foot. This creates a tidy, swift transition. Additional footwork must be avoided. The shoulders must remain at the same height in most movements from one step to the next. Bouncing up and down by bending the knees must be avoided.
- Bending the knee: Front kick must be executed by bending the knee before and after the kick. This assists balance and

the maintenance of a good posture or shape. This avoids the appearance of dropping the leg after the kick is executed, with lack of control and concentration.
- Power: Many practitioners are able to finish a pattern strongly with speed and power, but lack the same quality at the start of patterns. This is encouraged by the fact that patterns start with a defensive action; for example, a low section block, which is more difficult to produce power. The end of patterns consists of offensive actions such as a middle section punch, which is easier to generate speed and power. Practitioners must be aware of this criterion and generate the same degree of effort at the start of and throughout the whole routine.

Attending for promotion tests is not easy and many practitioners become nervous, which negatively affects performance. Absentmindedness can lead to mistakes and can affect even the most confident practitioner. Practitioners must always warm up before examinations, rehearse their routines to refresh the memory and focus 100 per cent on the task in hand. Routines must be repeated, drilled until they become habitual. Practitioners must aim to deliver the perfect pattern with power in order to earn promotion.

Training continues.

Chapter 13

Taegeuk patterns 1-8 Arrangement

Taegeuk pattern 1

1 Jang - Heaven and Light

Start: Ready stance, facing north.

1. Turn left 90° (move left foot), walking stance, low block.
2. Move forward, walking stance, middle punch.
3. Turn right 180° (move right foot), walking stance, low block.
4. Move forward, walking stance, middle punch.
5. Turn left 90° (move left foot), forward stance, low block.
6. Stationary, reverse middle punch.
7. Turn right 90° (move right foot), walking stance, reverse inner block.
8. Move forward, walking stance, reverse middle punch.
9. Turn left 180° (move left foot), walking stance, reverse inner block.
10. Move forward, walking stance, reverse middle punch.

11. Turn right 90° (move right foot), forward stance, low block.
12. Stationary, reverse middle punch.
13. Turn left 90° (move left foot), walking stance, high block.
14. Move forward, front kick, walking stance, middle punch.
15. Turn right 180° (move right foot), walking stance, high block.
16. Move forward, front kick, walking stance, middle punch.
17. Turn right 90° (move left foot), forward stance, low block.
18. Move forward, forward stance, middle punch (kihap).

End: Form a ready stance. Turn left 180°, pivot on the ball of the right foot and draw the left foot back.

_____   Notes   _____

Steps 5-6, 11 and 12 and 17 and 18
These actions must be performed swiftly and continuously.

Notes

Taegeuk Pattern 1 (18 Steps)

143

Stop

Kihap

18

18 Side

17

17 Side

Taegeuk Pattern 2

2 Jang - Joyfulness

Start: Ready stance, facing north.

1. Turn left 90° (move left foot), walking stance, low block.
2. Move forward, forward stance, middle punch.
3. Turn right 180° (move right foot), walking stance, low block.
4. Move forward, forward stance, middle punch.
5. Turn left 90° (move left foot), walking stance, reverse inner block.
6. Move forward, walking stance, reverse inner block.
7. Turn left 90° (move left foot), walking stance, low block.
8. Move forward, front kick, forward stance, high punch.
9. Turn right 180° (move right foot), walking stance, low block.
10. Move forward, front kick, forward stance, high punch.
11. Turn left 90° (move left foot), walking stance, high block.
12. Move forward, walking stance, high block.
13. Turn left 270° (move left foot), walking stance, reverse inner block.
14. Turn right 180° (move right foot), walking stance, reverse inner block.
15. Turn left 90° (move left foot), walking stance, low block.
16. Move forward, front kick, walking stance, middle punch.
17. Move forward, front kick, walking stance, middle punch.
18. Move forward, front kick, walking stance, middle punch (kihap).

End: Form a ready stance. Turn left 180°, pivot on the ball of the right foot and draw the left foot back.

Notes

Steps 16, 17 and 18
These actions must be performed swiftly and continuously.

Taegeuk Pattern 2 (18 Steps)

Start

1

2

4

3

5

6

7

8-1

149

17-1

17-1 Side

16-2

16-2 Side

16-1

16-1 Side

15

15 Side

Stop

Kihap

18-2

18-2 Side

18-1

18-1 Side

17-2

17-2 Side

Taegeuk Pattern 3

3 Jang - Fire and Sun

Start: Ready stance, facing north.

1. Turn left 90° (move left foot), walking stance, low block.
2. Move forward, front kick, forward stance, middle punch, reverse middle punch.
3. Turn right 180° (move right foot), walking stance, low block.
4. Move forward, front kick, forward stance, middle punch, reverse middle punch.
5. Turn left 90° (move left foot), walking stance, reverse inner knife-hand strike.
6. Move forward, walking stance, reverse inner knife-hand strike.
7. Turn left 90° (move left foot), back stance, knife-hand block.
8. Stationary, slide the left foot forward, forward stance, reverse middle punch.
9. Turn right 180° (move right foot), back stance, knife-hand block.
10. Stationary, slide the right foot forward, forward stance, reverse middle punch.
11. Turn left 90° (move left foot), walking stance, reverse inner block.
12. Move forward, walking stance, reverse inner block.
13. Turn left 270° (move left foot), walking stance, low block.
14. Move forward, front kick, forward stance, middle punch, reverse middle punch.
15. Turn right 180° (move right foot), walking stance, low block.
16. Move forward, front kick, forward stance, middle punch, reverse middle punch.
17. Turn left 90° (move left foot), walking stance, low block, reverse middle punch.

18. Move forward, walking stance, low block, reverse middle punch.
19. Move forward, front kick, walking stance, low block, reverse middle punch.
20. Move forward, front kick, walking stance, low block, reverse middle punch (kihap).

End: Form a ready stance. Turn left 180°, pivot on the ball of the right foot and draw the left foot back.

_____   Notes   _____

Steps 7 and 8, 9 and 10 and 17-20
These actions must be performed swiftly and continuously.

Steps 7 and 9
The knife-hand block must be performed on the outside of the reaction hand.

Notes

Taegeuk Pattern 3 (20 Steps)

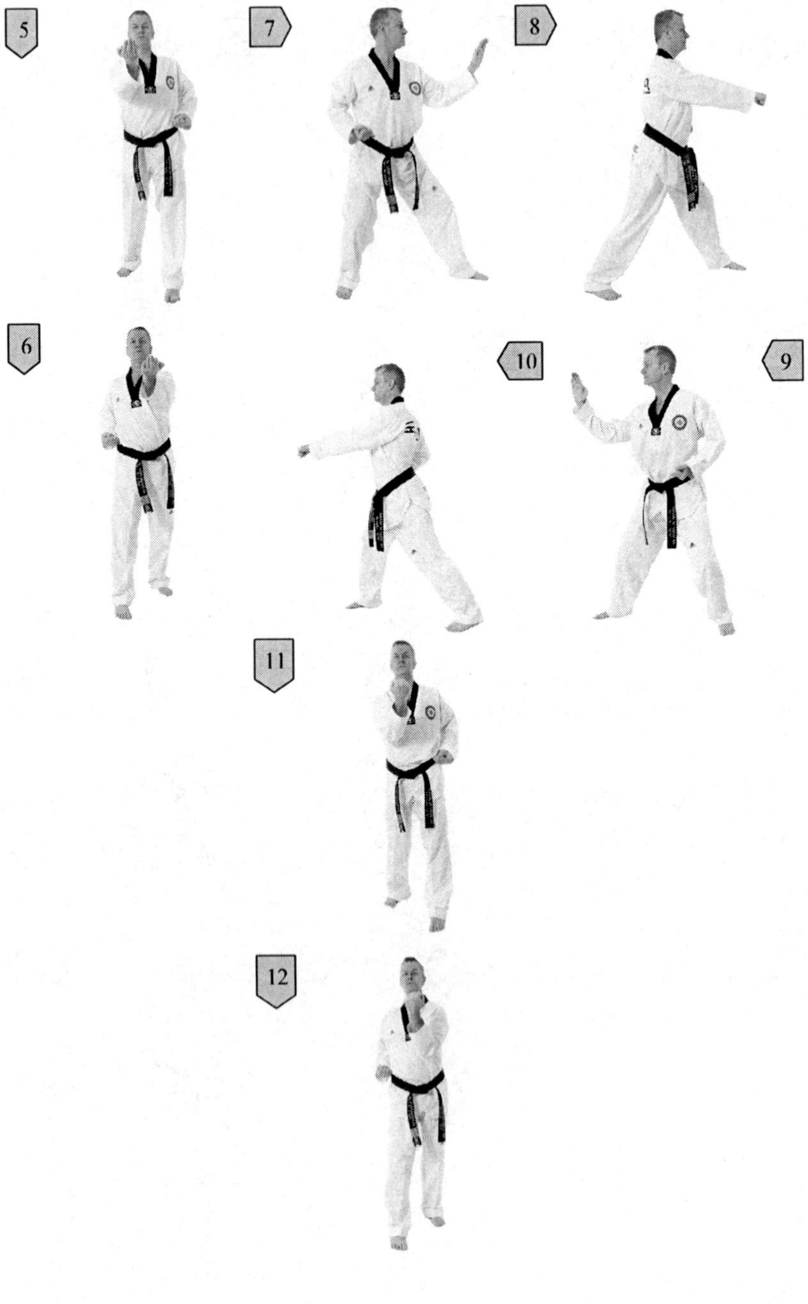
5
7
8
6
10
9
11
12

157

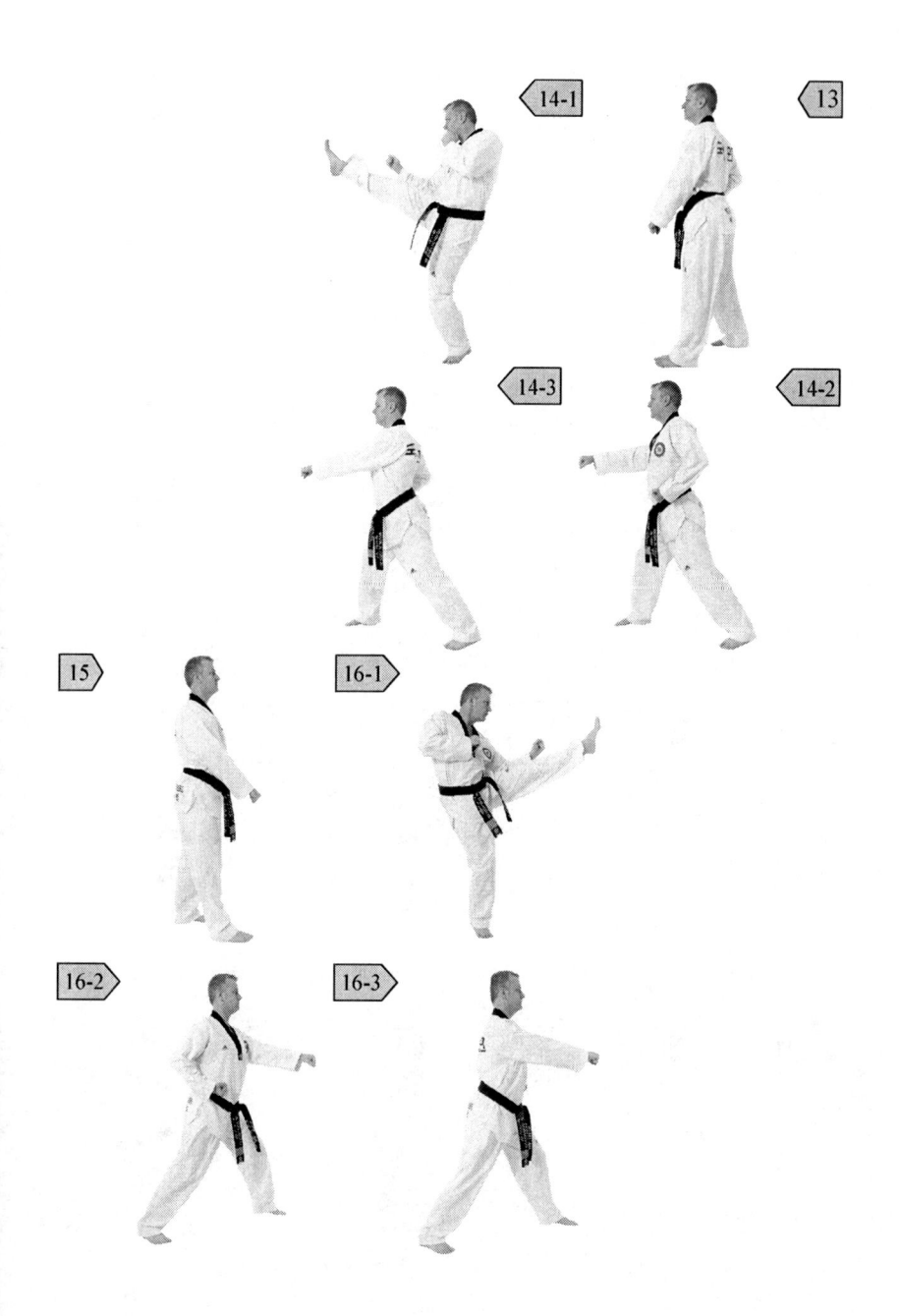

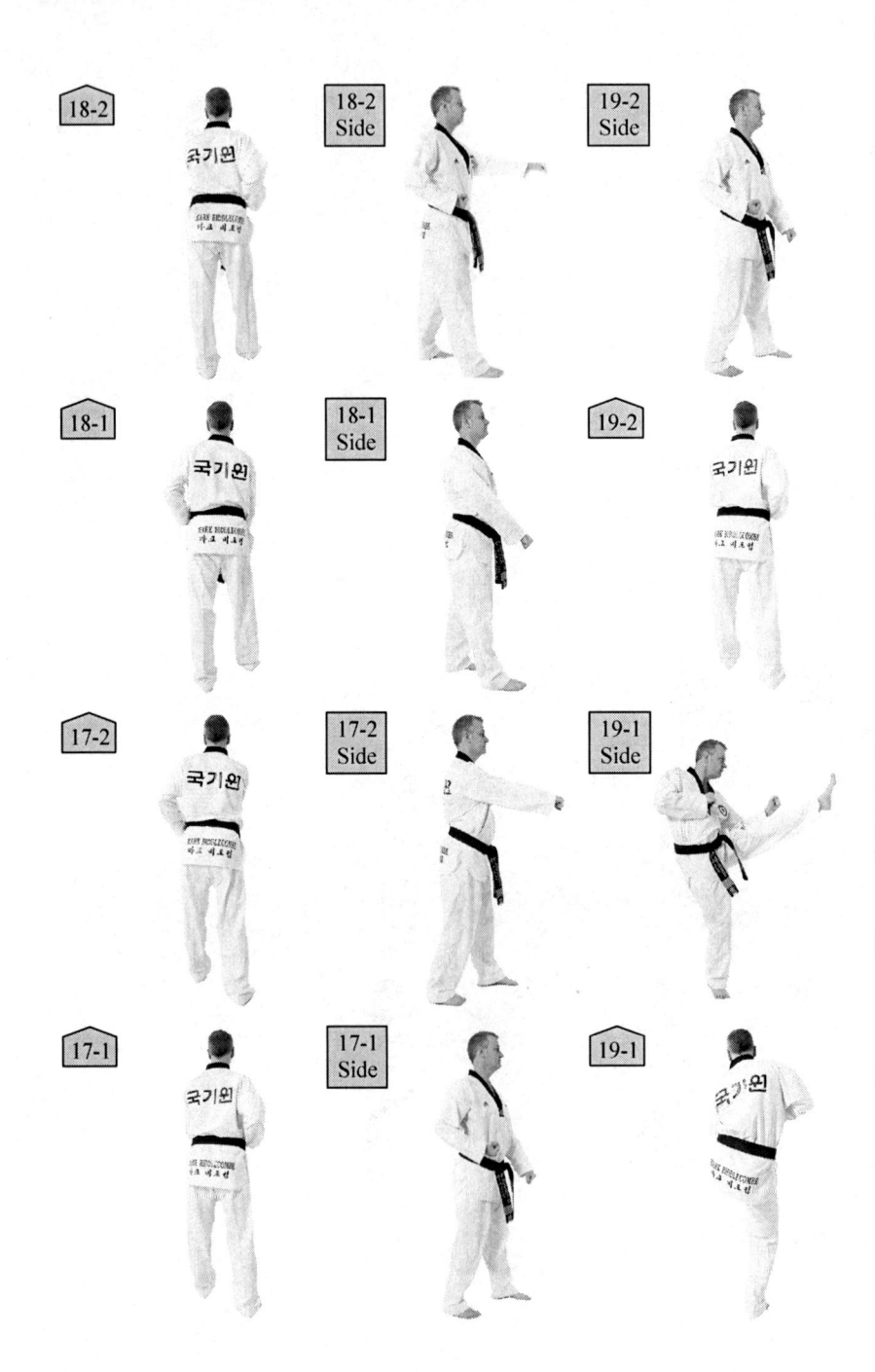

18-2		18-2 Side		19-2 Side	
18-1		18-1 Side		19-2	
17-2		17-2 Side		19-1 Side	
17-1		17-1 Side		19-1	

20-3		20-3 Side		Stop	

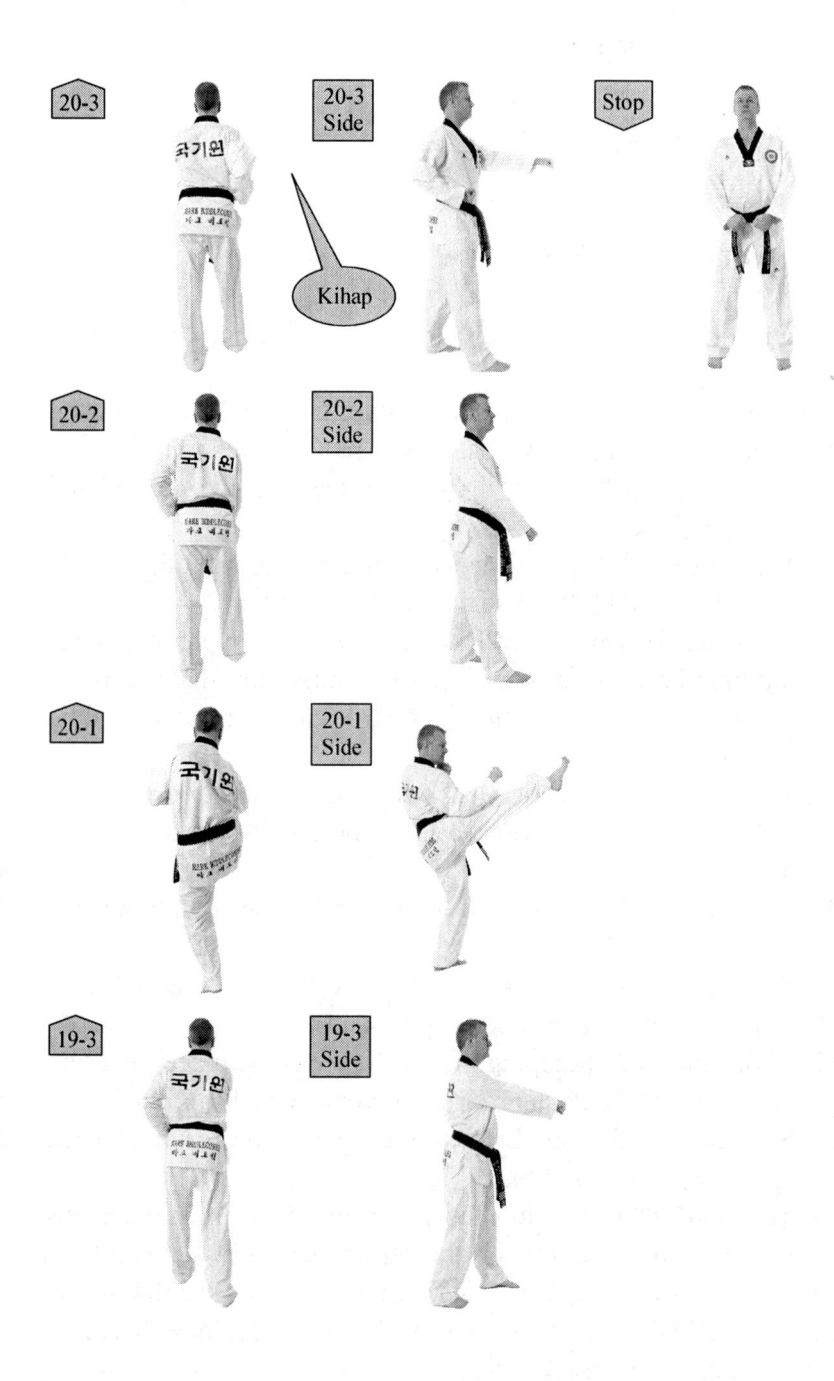

Kihap

20-2		20-2 Side	

20-1		20-1 Side	

19-3		19-3 Side	

Taegeuk Pattern 4

4 Jang - Thunder and Lightning

Start: Ready stance, facing north.

1. Turn left 90° (move left foot), back stance, knife-hand guarding block.
2. Move forward, forward stance, simultaneous left downward palm block and right vertical spear-hand strike.
3. Turn right 180° (move right foot), back stance, knife-hand guarding block.
4. Move forward, forward stance, simultaneous right downward palm block and left vertical spear-hand strike.
5. Turn left 90° (move left foot), forward stance, simultaneous left high knife-hand block and right inner knife-hand strike.
6. Move forward, front kick, forward stance, reverse middle punch.
7. Move forward, side kick, back stance, guarding block.
8. Move forward, side kick, back stance, knife-hand guarding block.
9. Turn left 270° (move left foot), back stance, left reverse outerform block.
10. Stationary, right front kick, replacing into the original back stance, reverse inner block (right hand).
11. Turn right 180° (keeping the feet at the same place, pivoting on the heels), back stance, right reverse outerform block.
12. Stationary, left front kick, replacing into the original back stance, reverse inner block (left hand).
13. Turn left 90° (move left foot), forward stance, simultaneous left high knife-hand block and right inner knife-hand strike.
14. Move forward, front kick, forward stance, front backfist strike.
15. Turn left 90° (move left foot), walking stance, inner block.
16. Stationary, reverse middle punch.

17. Turn right 180° (keeping the feet at the same place, pivoting on the heels), walking stance, inner block.
18. Stationary, reverse middle punch.
19. Turn left 90° (move left foot), forward stance, inner block, reverse middle punch, middle punch.
20. Move forward, forward stance, inner block, reverse middle punch, middle punch (kihap).

End: Form a ready stance. Turn left 180°, pivot on the ball of the right foot and draw the left foot back.

_____ Notes _____

Steps 7 and 8
These actions must be performed swiftly and continuously.

Notes

Taegeuk Pattern 4 (20 Steps)

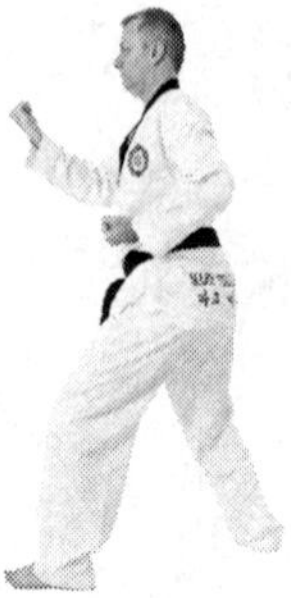

10-2

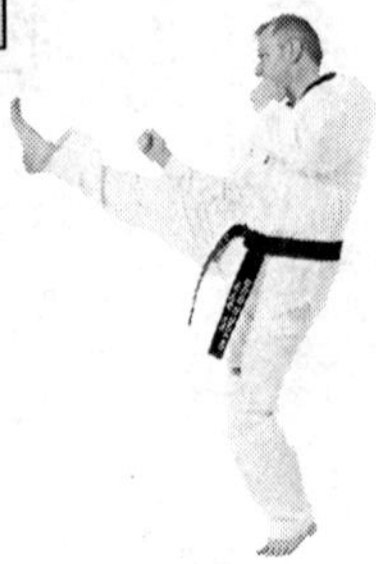

10-1

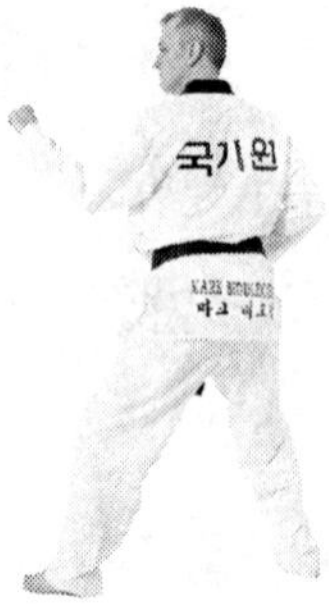

9

11

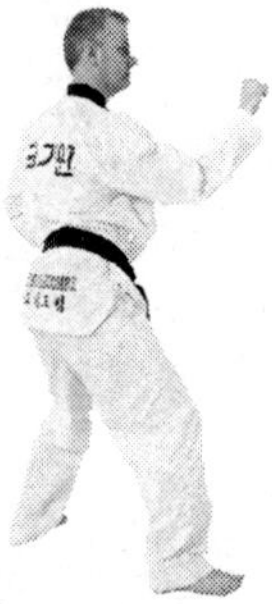

12-1

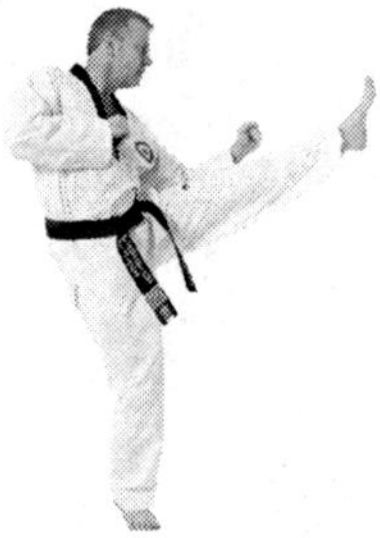

12-2

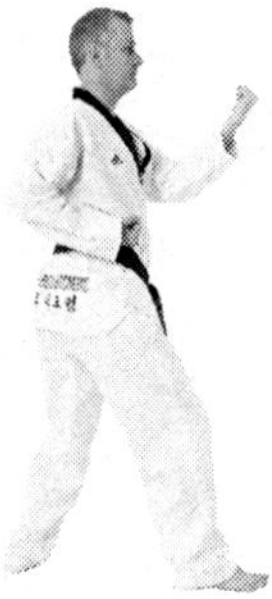

14-1

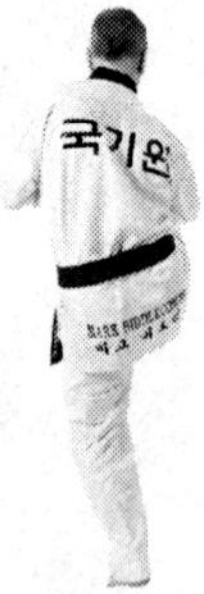

14-1 Side

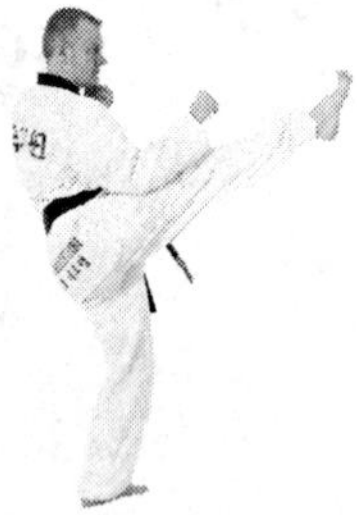

13

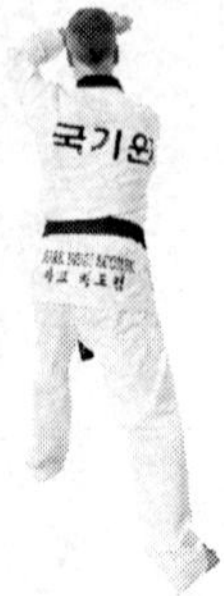

13 Side

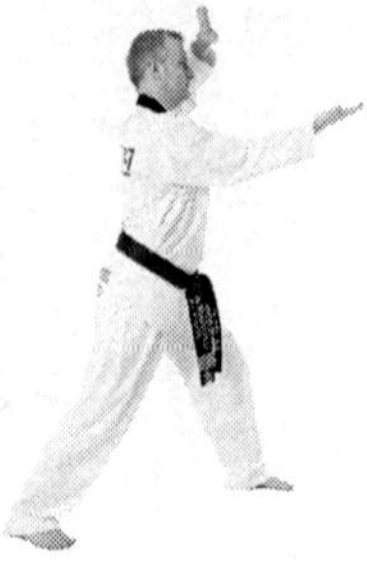

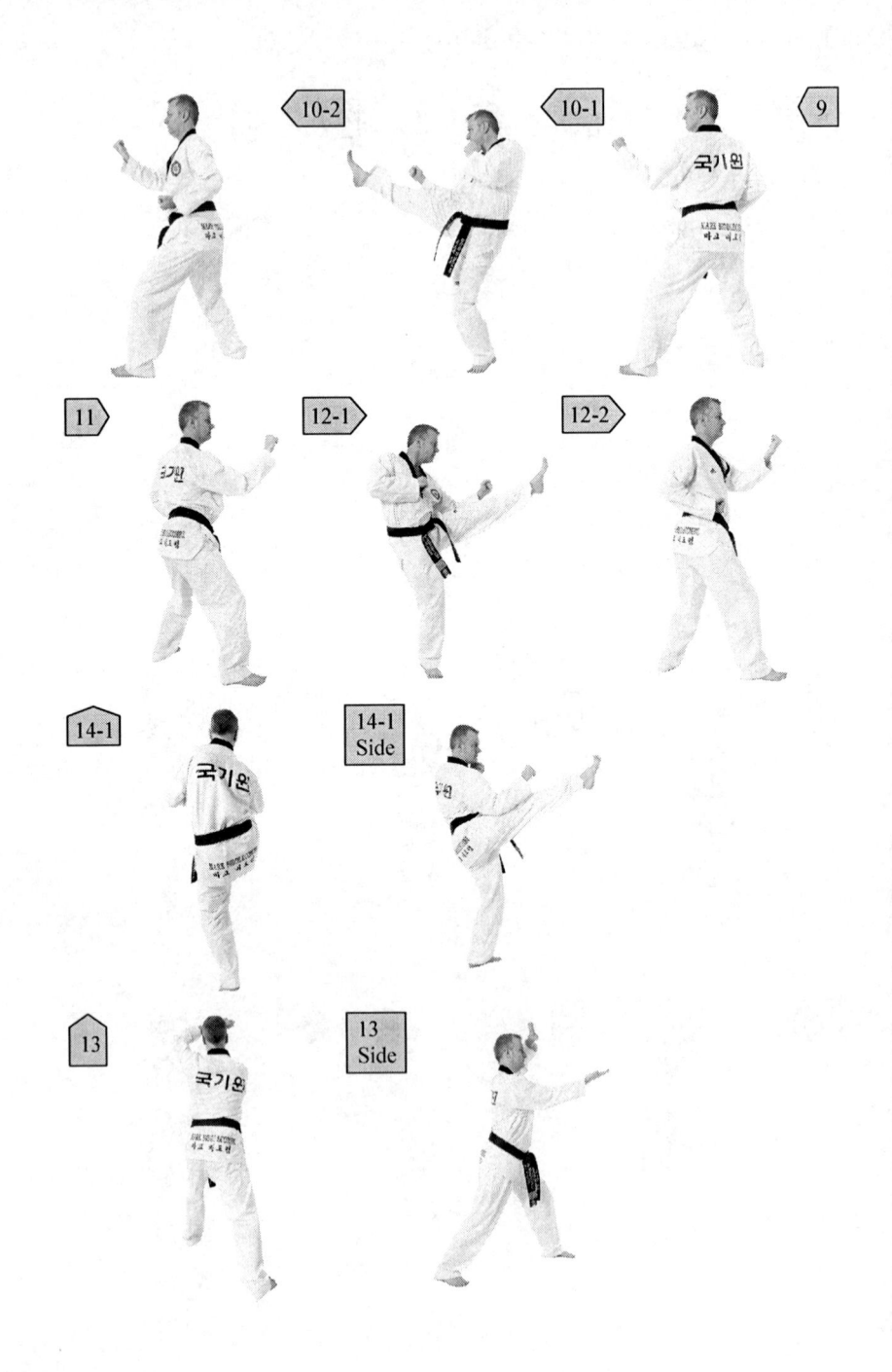

165

Taegeuk Pattern 5

5 Jang - Wind

Start: Ready stance, facing north.

1. Turn left 90° (move left foot), forward stance, low block.
2. Stationary, pull left foot back, 'L'-shaped stance, hammer-fist strike.
3. Turn right 180° (move right foot), forward stance, low block.
4. Stationary, pull right foot back, 'L'-shaped stance, hammer-fist strike.
5. Turn left 90° (move left foot), forward stance, inner block, reverse inner block.
6. Move forward, front kick, forward stance, front backfist strike, reverse inner block.
7. Move forward, front kick, forward stance, front backfist strike, reverse inner block.
8. Move forward, forward stance, front backfist strike.
9. Turn left 270° (move left foot), back stance, left knife-hand block.
10. Move forward, forward stance, horizontal elbow strike (place the right fist into the left hand).
11. Turn right 180° (move right foot), back stance, right knife-hand block.
12. Move forward, forward stance, horizontal elbow strike (place the left fist into the right hand).
13. Turn left 90° (move left foot), forward stance, low block, reverse inner block.
14. Move forward, front kick, forward stance, low block, reverse inner block.
15. Turn left 90° (move left foot), forward stance, high block.
16. Move forward, simultaneous side kick and side hammer-fist strike, forward stance, reverse horizontal target elbow strike.

17. Turn right 180° (move right foot), forward stance, high block.
18. Move forward, simultaneous side kick and side hammer-fist strike, forward stance, reverse horizontal target elbow strike.
19. Turn left 90° (move left foot), forward stance, low block, reverse inner block.
20. Move forward, front kick, cross-legged stance, front backfist strike (kihap).

End: Form a ready stance. Turn left 180°, pivot on the ball of the right foot and move the left foot out.

_____   Notes   _____

Steps 2 and 4
The hammer-fist strike must be performed on the inside of the reaction hand.

Notes

Taegeuk Pattern 5   (20 Steps)

6-2

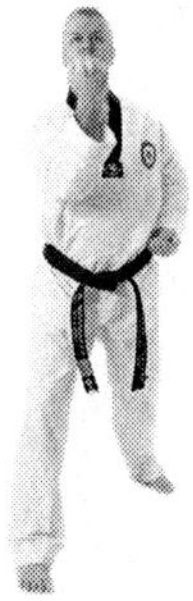

7-1

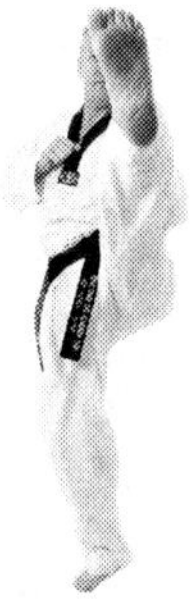

7-3

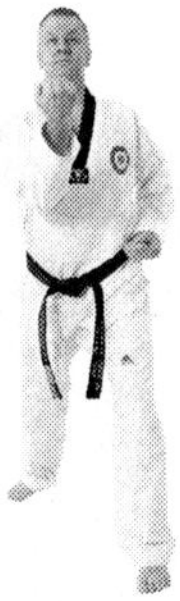

6-3

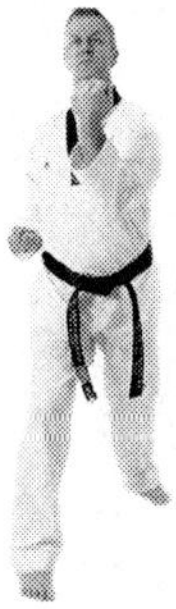

7-2

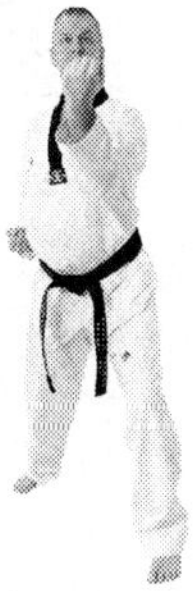

8

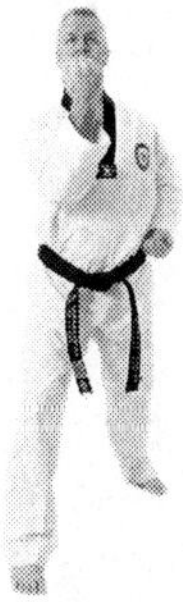

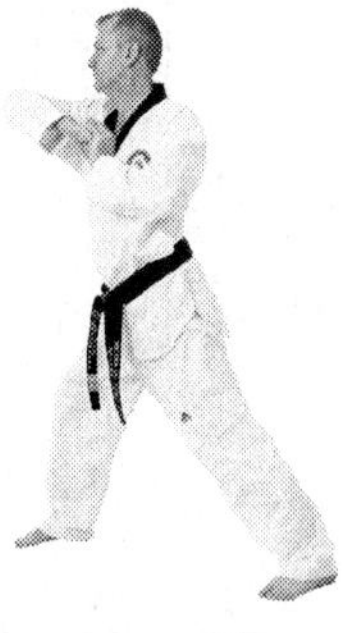

10

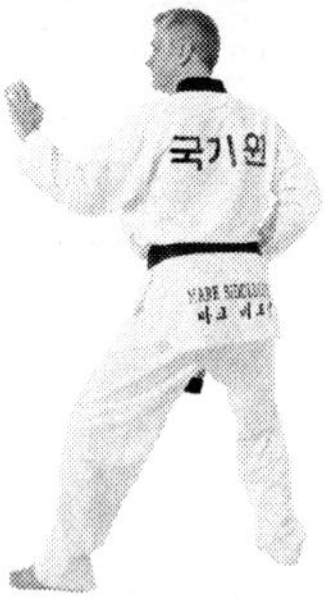

9

11

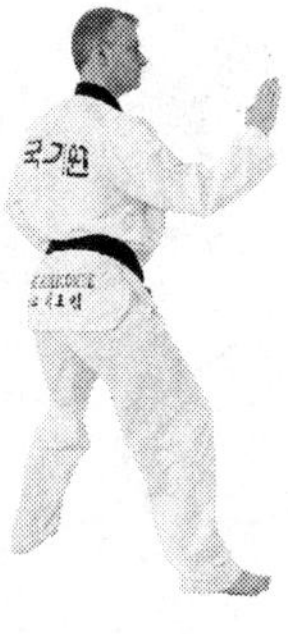

12

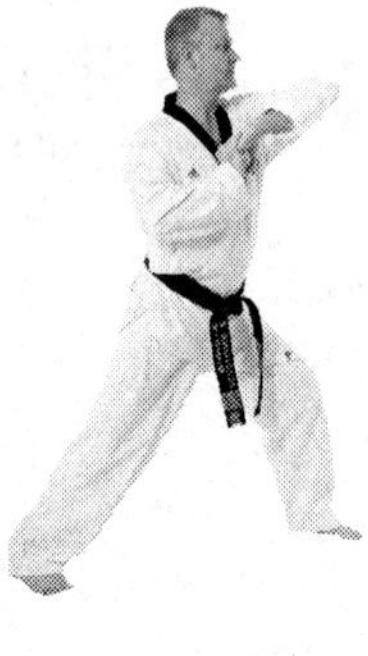

14-2

14-2 Side

14-1

14-1 Side

13-2

13-2 Side

13-1

13-1 Side

18-1

18-2

17

16-2

16-1

15

14-3

14-3 Side

173

174

Taegeuk Pattern 6

6 Jang - Water

Start: Ready stance, facing north.

1. Turn left 90° (move left foot), forward stance, low block.
2. Stationary, right front kick, returning the kicking foot to its original position and pulling the front foot back slightly, back stance, reverse outerform block (left hand).
3. Turn right 180° (move right foot), forward stance, low block.
4. Stationary, left front kick, returning the kicking foot to its original position and pulling the front foot back slightly, back stance, reverse outerform block (right hand).
5. Turn left 90° (move left foot), forward stance, right knife-hand block (face height).
6. Move forward, roundhouse kick, forward stance, then turn left 90° (move left foot), forward stance, reverse outerform block (left hand at face height) and reverse middle punch.
7. Move forward, front kick, forward stance, reverse middle punch.
8. Turn right 180° (move right foot), forward stance, reverse outerform block (right hand at face height) and reverse middle punch.
9. Move forward, front kick, forward stance, reverse middle punch.
10. Turn left 90° (move left foot), ready stance, twin low-section block (performed with force, approximately 5 seconds).
11. Move forward (move right foot), forward stance, left knife-hand block (face height).
12. Move forward, roundhouse kick (kihap), with the left foot still in the air pivot on the right foot so that the body turns 180° facing south, place the left foot behind to form a right forward stance, then turn right 90° (move right foot), forward

stance, low block.
13. Stationary, left front kick, returning the kicking foot to its original position and pulling the front foot back slightly, back stance, reverse outerform block (right hand).
14. Turn left 180° (move left foot), forward stance, low block.
15. Stationary, right front kick, returning the kicking foot to its original position and pulling the front foot back slightly, back stance, reverse outerform block (left hand).
16. Turn left 90° (move right foot), back stance, knife-hand guarding block.
17. Move backwards (move left foot), back stance, knife-hand guarding block.
18. Move backwards (move right foot), forward stance, inner palm block, reverse middle punch.
19. Move backwards (move left foot), forward stance, inner palm block, reverse middle punch.

End: Form a ready stance. Pull the right foot back.

Notes

Steps 2, 4, 13 and 15
Once the front kick has been executed, the kicking foot must land on the floor at the same time as executing the reverse outerform block.

Step 10
On set-up, the forearms must cross over at chest height with left arm placed on the outside. The right arm is positioned on the inside - between the left arm and the body.

Taegeuk Pattern 6 (19 Steps)

Kihap

181

Taegeuk Pattern 7

7 Jang - Mountain

Start: Ready stance, facing north.

1. Turn left 90° (move left foot), cat stance, reverse inner palm block.
2. Stationary, right front kick and returning the kicking foot to its original position, inner block.
3. Turn right 180° (move right foot), cat stance, reverse inner palm block.
4. Stationary, left front kick and returning the kicking foot to its original position, inner block.
5. Turn left 90° (move left foot), back stance, low knife-hand guarding block.
6. Move forward, back stance, low knife-hand guarding block.
7. Turn left 90° (move left foot), cat stance, reverse inner palm block (simultaneously place the left fist under the right elbow).
8. Stationary, reverse front backfist strike.
9. Turn right 180° (move right foot), cat stance, reverse inner palm block (simultaneously place the right fist under the left elbow).
10. Stationary, reverse front backfist strike.
11. Turn left 90° (move left foot), close stance, covering-fist (performed in slow motion, approximately 5 seconds).
12. Move forward (move left foot), forward stance, scissors block (left outerform block, right low block), scissors block (left low block, right outerform block).
13. Move forward, forward stance, scissors block (right outerform block, left low block), scissors block (right low block, left outerform block).
14. Turn left 270° (move left foot), forward stance, wedge block.
15. Stationary, reach forward and grasp the opponent's head,

palms open, then move forward, clench the hands into fists and simultaneously pull the hands down towards the ankle and execute a knee attack, cross-legged stance, twin upset punch.
16. Stationary, slide left foot back, forward stance, low 'X' block. The action must be set up at the left side of the waist.
17. Turn right 180° (move right foot), forward stance, wedge block.
18. Stationary, reach forward and grasp the opponent's head, palms open, then move forward, clench the hands into fists and simultaneously pull the hands down towards the ankle and execute a knee attack, cross-legged stance, twin upset punch.
19. Stationary, slide right foot back, forward stance, low 'X' block. The action must be set up at the right side of the waist.
20. Turn left 90° (move left foot), walking stance, side backfist strike.
21. Move forward, inner crescent target kick (striking the palm of the left hand), side horse riding stance and horizontal target elbow strike.
22. Stationary, slide left foot up slightly behind the right foot, walking stance, side backfist strike.
23. Move forward, inner crescent target kick (striking the palm of the right hand), side horse riding stance and horizontal target elbow strike.
24. Stationary, side knife-hand block.
25. Move forward, side horse riding stance, side middle punch (kihap).

End: Form a ready stance. Turn the body left 90°, pivot on the ball of the right foot and draw the left foot back.

Notes

Steps 2 and 4
Once the front kick has been executed, the kicking foot must land on the floor at the same time as executing the inner block.

Step 11
The movement is set up at the lower abdomen and executed at the height of the philtrum.

Notes

Taegeuk Pattern 7   (25 Steps)

11

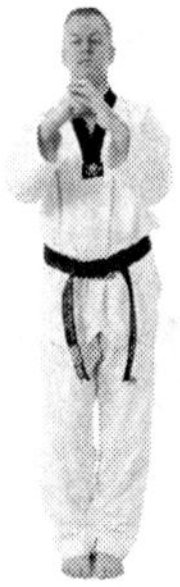

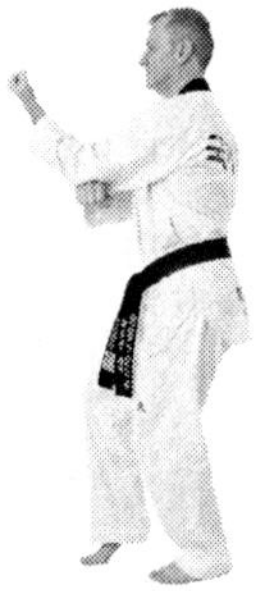

10

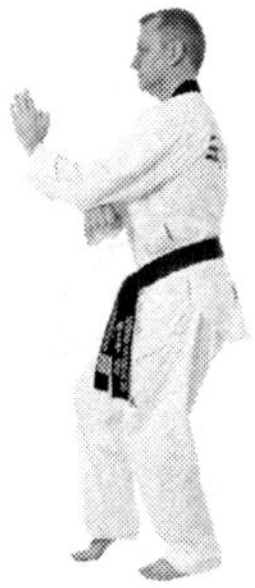

9

12-1

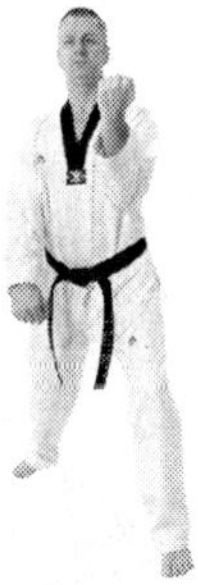

13-1

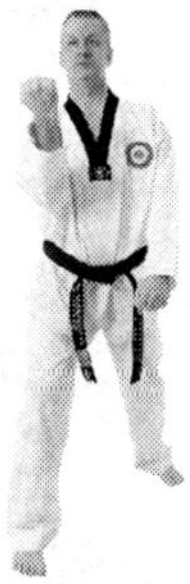

12-2

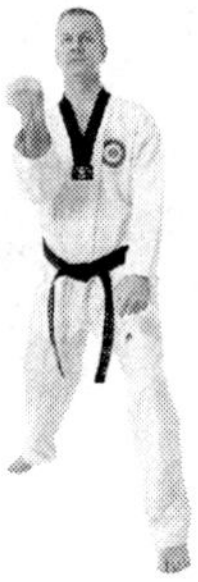

13-2

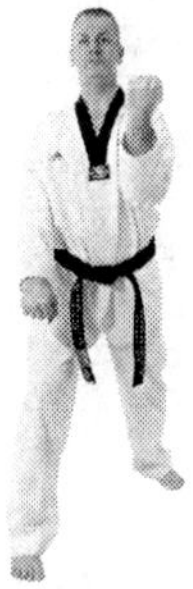

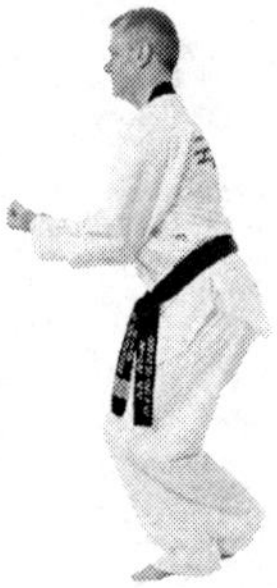

15-2

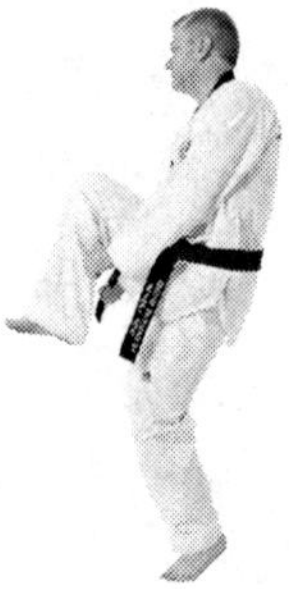

15-1

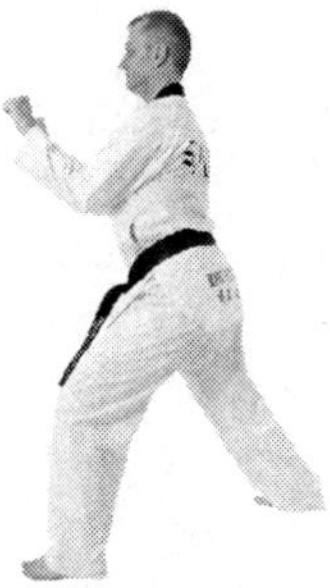

14

17

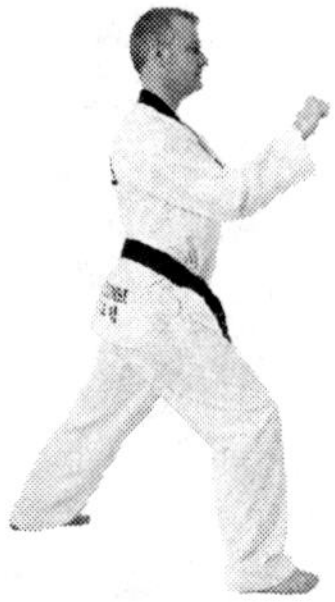

16

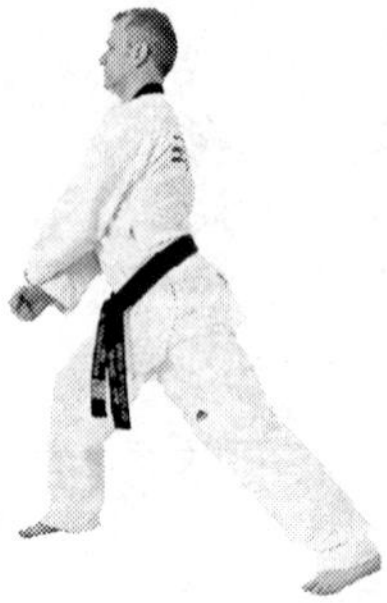

18-1

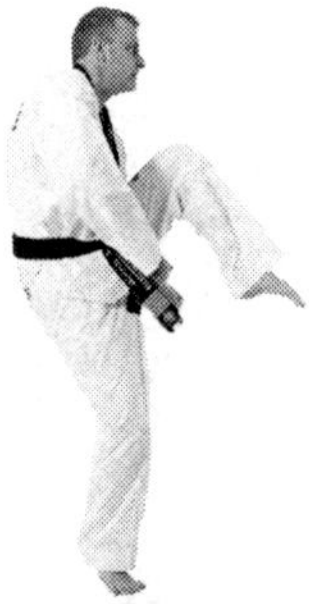

18-2

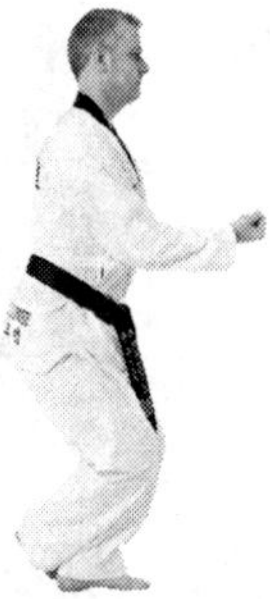

19

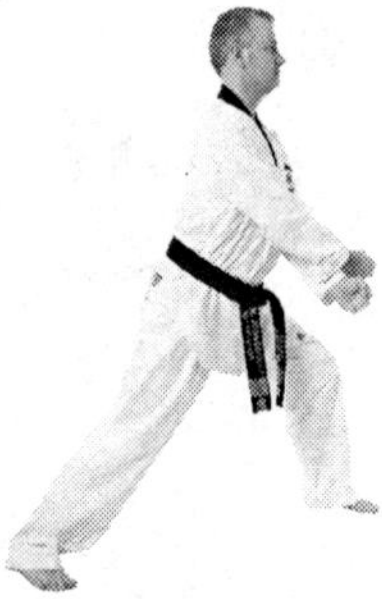

21-1

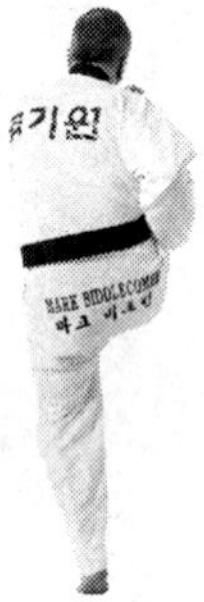

21-1 Side

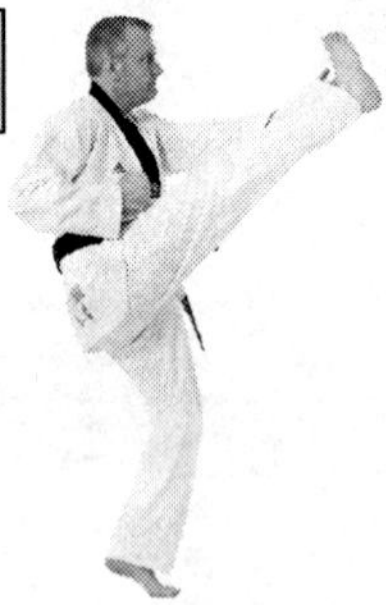

21-2 Side

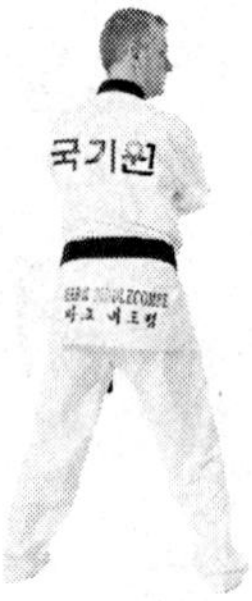

20

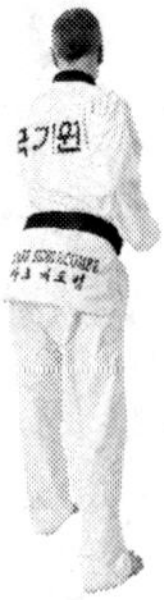

20 Side

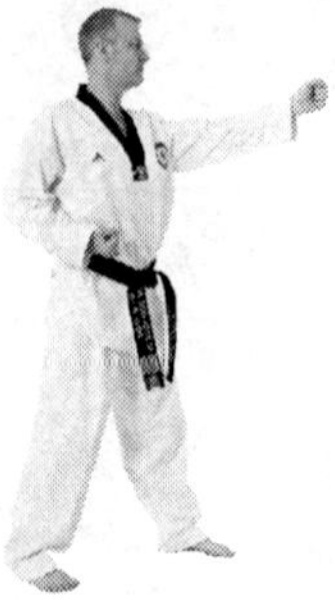

21-2

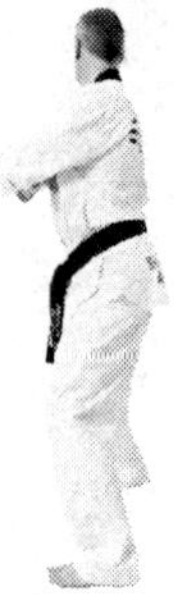

189

Taegeuk Pattern 8

8 Jang - Earth

Start: Ready stance, facing north.

1. Move forward (move left foot), back stance, guarding block.
2. Slide left foot forward slightly, forward stance, reverse middle punch.
3. Move forward, jumping double front kick; right then left in quick succession (kihap), forward stance, inner block, reverse middle punch, middle punch.
4. Move forward, forward stance, middle punch.
5. Looking over your left shoulder, turn the body left 90° (move left foot), forward stance (with the body facing west and the eyes looking east), half mountain block (left low block, right outerform block at face height).
6. Stationary, turn the body 180° to the left (both feet remain at the same place and pivot slightly), forward stance, simultaneous right uppercut punch and place the left fist on to the right shoulder (performed with force, approximately 8 seconds).
7. Turn right 180° (move the left foot in front of the right foot), cross-legged stance, and then step out with the right foot, forward stance (with the body facing east and the eyes looking west), half mountain block (right low block, left outerform block at face height).
8. Stationary, turn the body 180° to the right (both feet remain at the same place and pivot slightly), forward stance, simultaneous left uppercut punch and place the right fist on to the left shoulder (performed with force, approximately 8 seconds).
9. Turn left 270° (move right foot), back stance, knife-hand guarding block.

10. Slide left foot forward slightly, forward stance, reverse middle punch.
11. Stationary, right front kick, returning the kicking foot to its original position, then move backwards (move the left foot behind the right foot), cat stance, inner palm block.
12. Turn left 90° (move left foot), cat stance, knife-hand guarding block.
13. Move forward, left front kick, forward stance, reverse middle punch.
14. Stationary, pull the left foot back slightly, cat stance, inner palm block.
15. Turn right 180° (move right foot), cat stance, knife-hand guarding block.
16. Move forward, right front kick, forward stance, reverse middle punch.
17. Stationary, pull the right foot back slightly, cat stance, inner palm block.
18. Turn right 90° (move right foot), back stance, low guarding block.
19. Move forward, left front kick, while the left foot is still in the air, jumping right front kick (kihap), forward stance, inner block, reverse middle punch, middle punch.
20. Turn left 270° (move left foot), back stance, knife-hand block.
21. Stationary, slide the left foot forward, forward stance, reverse horizontal elbow strike (right elbow at chin height).
22. Stationary, reverse front backfist strike.
23. Stationary, left middle punch.
24. Turn right 180° (move right foot), back stance, knife-hand block.
25. Stationary, slide the right foot forward, forward stance, reverse horizontal elbow strike (left elbow at chin height).
26. Stationary, reverse front backfist strike.
27. Stationary, right middle punch.

End: Form a ready stance. Turn the body left 90°, pivot on the ball of the right foot and draw the left foot back.

Notes

Steps 5 and 7
Both feet on the forward stance must be pointing outward at 45 degrees.

Steps 22 and 26
The front backfist strike does not use a reaction hand to assist power.

Notes

Taegeuk Pattern 8 (27 Steps)

11-1

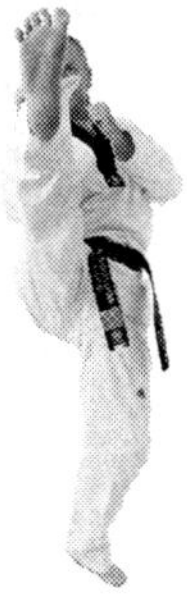

13-2

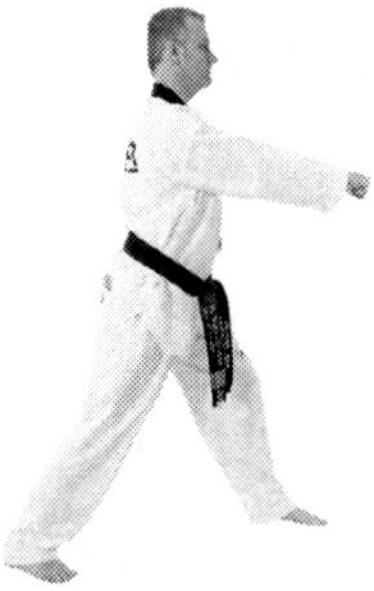

14

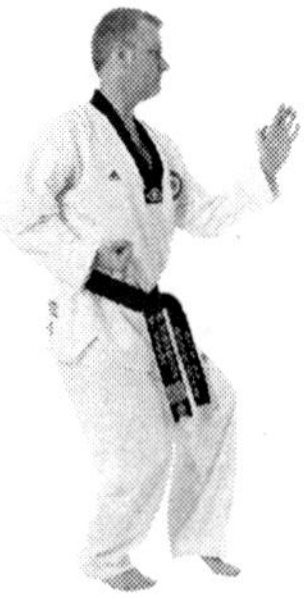

10

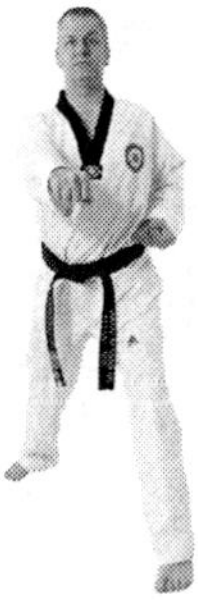

12

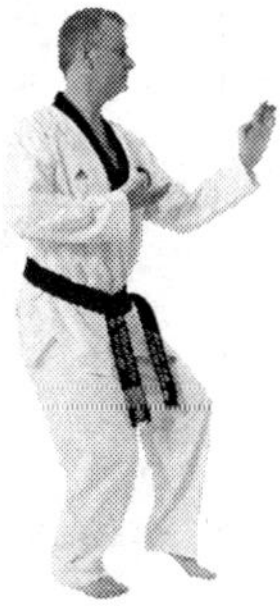

13-1

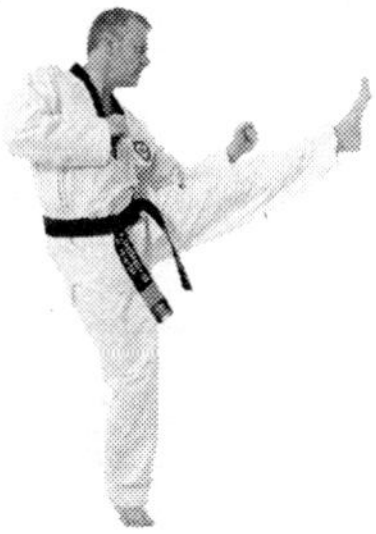

9

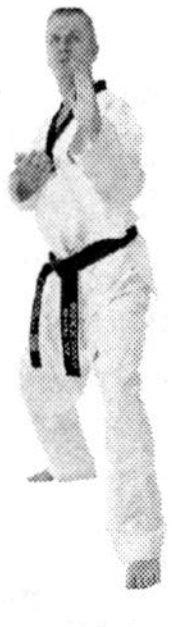

11-2

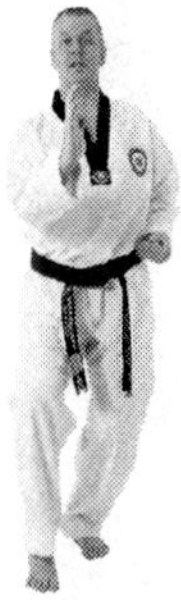

7-2

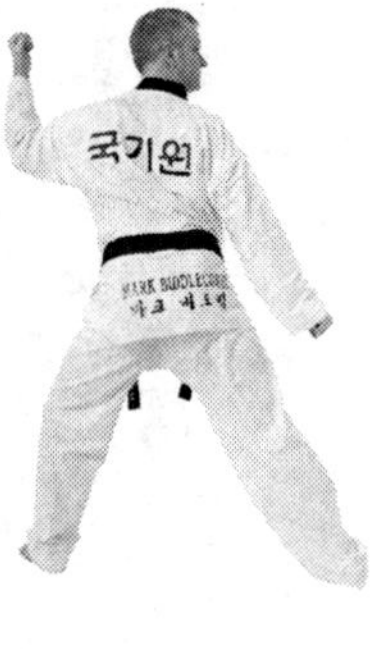

8

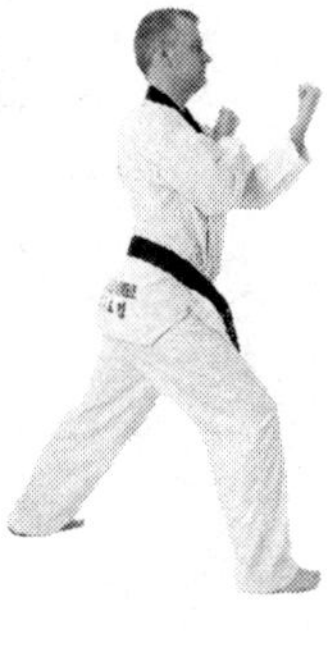

19-1

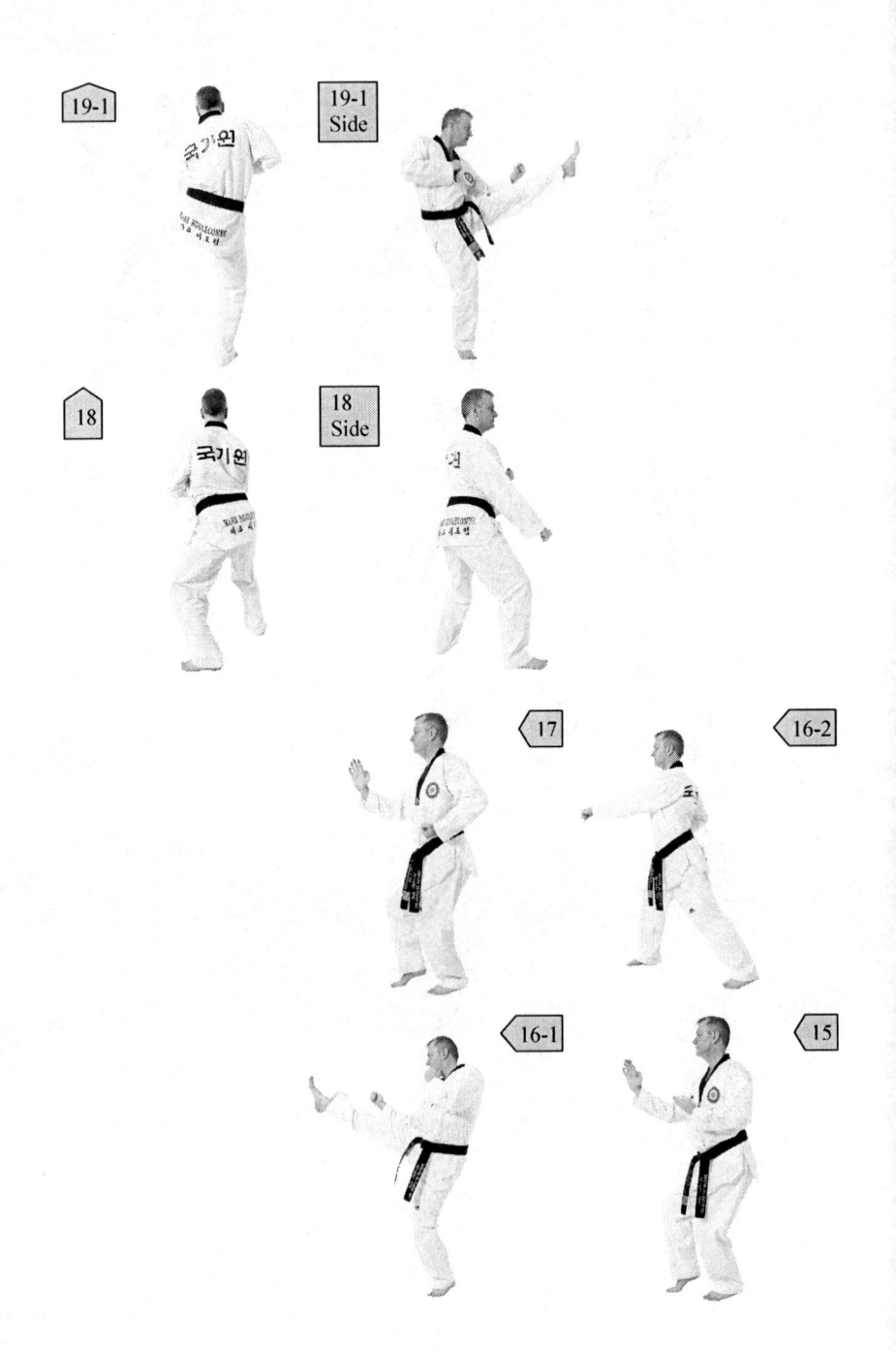

19-1 Side

18

18 Side

17

16-2

16-1

15

19-5

19-5 Side

19-4

19-4 Side

19-3

19-3 Side

Kihap

19-2

19-2 Side

197

20
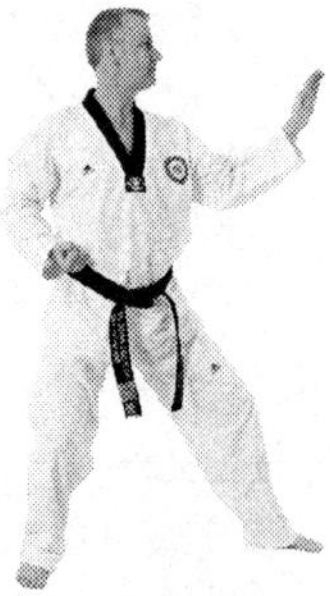

21
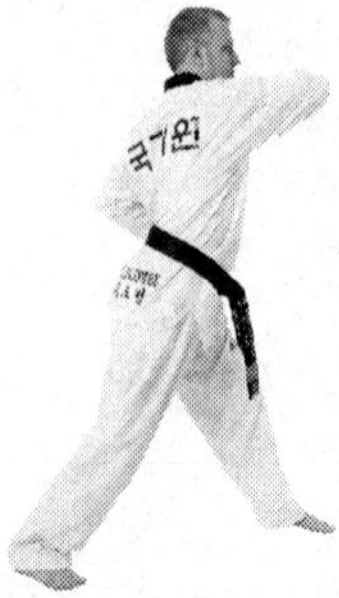

22
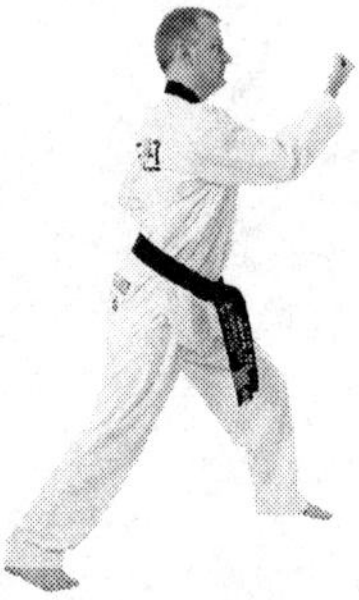

23
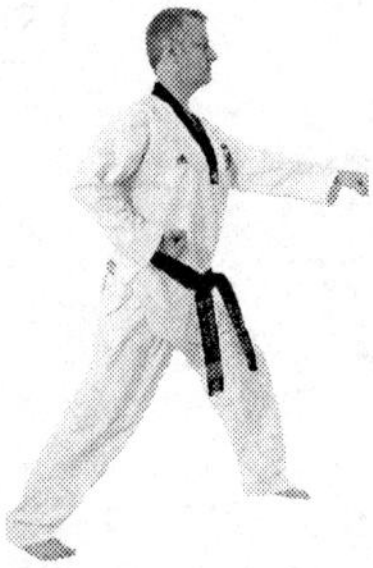

24
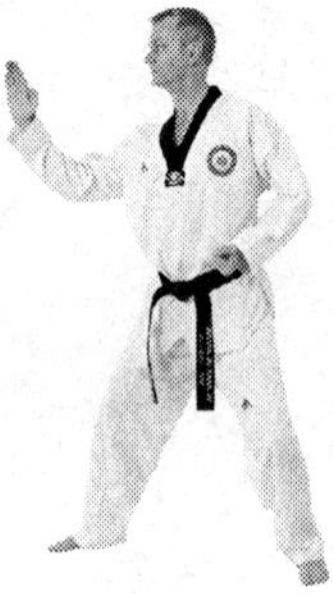

25
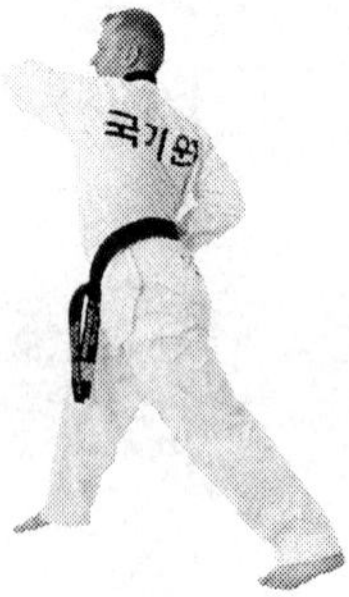

26
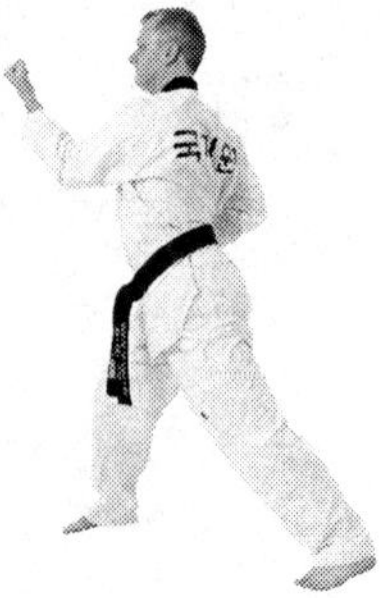

27
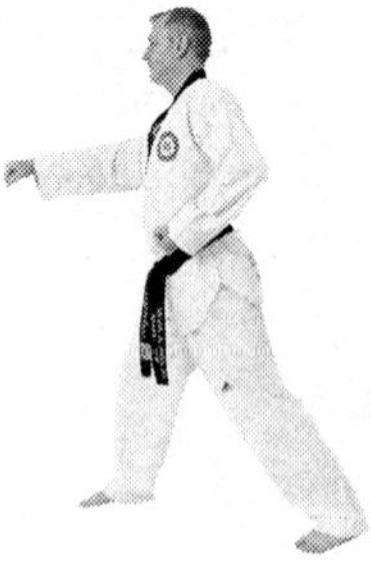

Stop
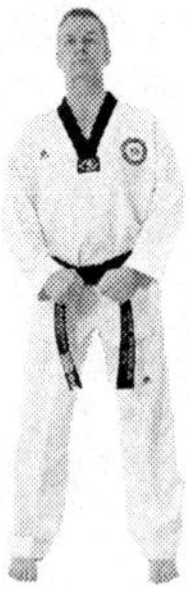

Chapter 14

Black belt patterns 1-9 Arrangement

Black Belt Pattern 1 - Koryo

Poomsae Koryo - Spirit

Start: Ready stance, barrel pushing (in slow motion), facing north.

1. Turn left 90° (move left foot), back stance, knife-hand guarding block.
2. Move forward, low/high side kick, forward stance, outer knife-hand strike.
3. Stationary, reverse middle punch.
4. Stationary, pull right foot back slightly, back stance, inner block.
5. Turn right 180° (move right foot), back stance, knife-hand guarding block.
6. Move forward, low/high side kick, forward stance, outer knife-hand strike.
7. Stationary, reverse middle punch.

8. Stationary, pull left foot back slightly, back stance, inner block.
9. Turn left 90° (move left foot), forward stance, low knife-hand block, reverse arc hand strike.
10. Move forward, front kick, forward stance, low knife-hand block, reverse arc hand strike.
11. Move forward, front kick, forward stance, low knife-hand block, reverse arc hand strike (kihap).
12. Move forward, front kick, forward stance, left downward arc hand strike (place the right hand underneath the left elbow with the palm facing up).
13. Move forward, and turn right 180° (step forward with the left foot and pivot on the right foot), forward stance, twin outerform block.
14. Move forward, front kick, forward stance, right downward arc hand strike (place the left hand underneath the right elbow with the palm facing up).
15. Stationary, pull the left foot back slightly, walking stance, twin outerform block.
16. Turn right 180° (move right foot), side horse riding stance (with the body facing north and the eye looking west), side knife-hand block.
17. Stationary, side target punch (right fist into the left palm).
18. Move forward (cross the right foot in front of the left foot), cross-legged stance, then simultaneously execute a left side kick whilst pulling your fists to the right side of the hip, land the foot forwards (west) and turn right 180° (pivot on right foot), forward stance (east). Simultaneous right hand scoop (place on left shoulder), left low spear-hand strike (both palms are facing up).
19. Stationary, pull right foot back slightly, walking stance, low block.
20. Move forward, walking stance, downward palm block. Move forward again, side horse riding stance, reinforced side thrust elbow strike.
21. Stationary, side knife-hand block.

22. Stationary, side target punch (left fist into the right palm).
23. Move forward (cross the left foot over right foot), cross-legged stance, then simultaneously execute a right side kick whilst pulling your fists to the left side of the hip, land the foot forwards (east) and turn left 180° (pivot on left foot), forward stance (west). Simultaneous left hand scoop (place on right shoulder), right low spear-hand strike (both palms are facing up).
24. Stationary, pull left foot back slightly, walking stance, low block.
25. Move forward, walking stance, downward palm block. Move forward again, side horse riding stance, reinforced side thrust elbow strike.
26. Turn right 90° (pull the right foot in, facing north), close stance, left hammer-fist target strike (performed in slow motion, approximately 5 seconds).
27. Turn left 180° (move left foot), forward stance, outer knife-hand strike, low knife-hand block (same hand).
28. Move forward, forward stance, inner knife-hand strike, low knife-hand block (same hand).
29. Move forward, forward stance, inner knife-hand strike, low knife-hand block (same hand).
30. Move forward, forward stance, arc hand strike (kihap).

End: Form a ready stance, barrel pushing (in slow motion). Turn left 180°, pivot on the ball of the right foot and draw the left foot back.

—

Notes

Ready Stance
Barrel pushing, position the finger tips at the height of the philtrum.

Steps 2 and 6
Execute the outer knife-hand strike and the forward stance simultaneously.

Step 26
The palms must be open above the head, making a large circular action, when the hands reach shoulder height the left hand is clenched, forming a fist.

Koryo (30 Steps)

Start | 1 | 2-1

2-2 | 2-3

3 | 4

6-1 | 5

6-2

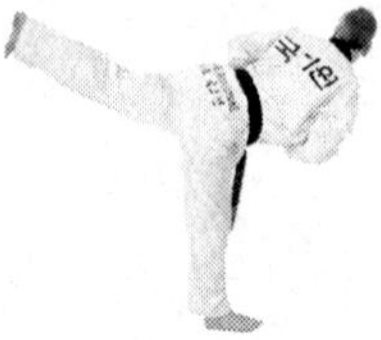

6-3

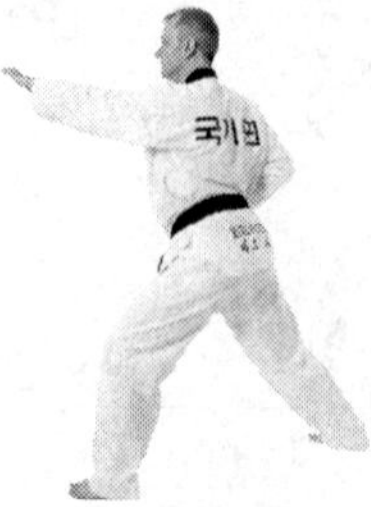

7

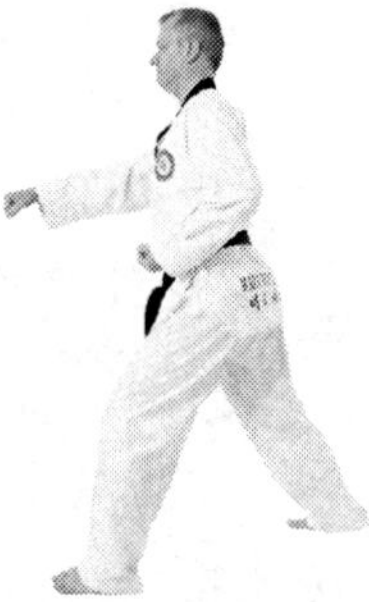

8

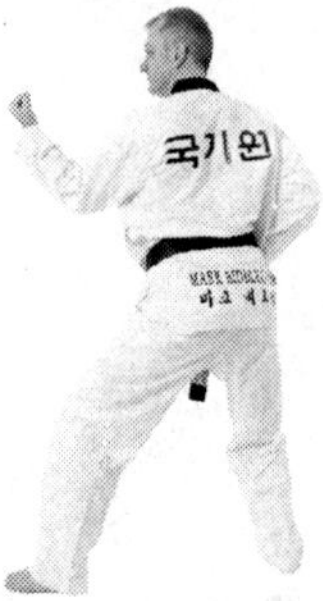

9-1

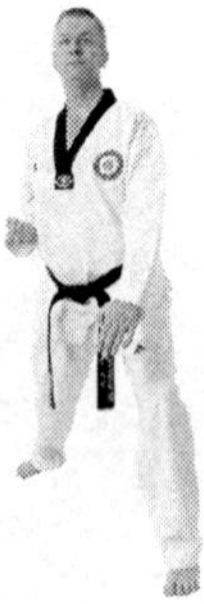

9-2

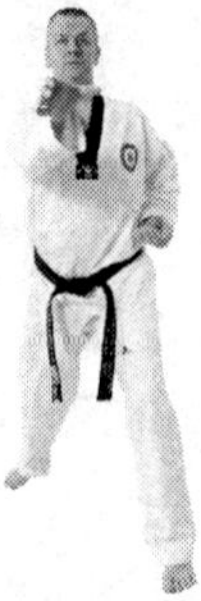

10-1

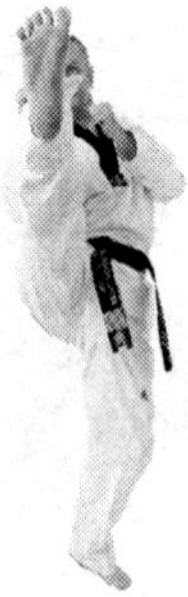

10-2

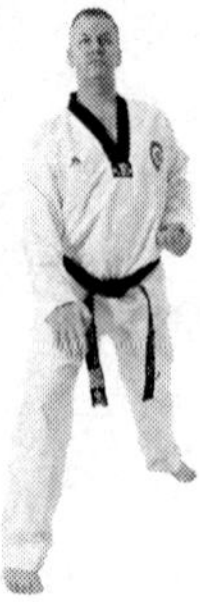

10-3

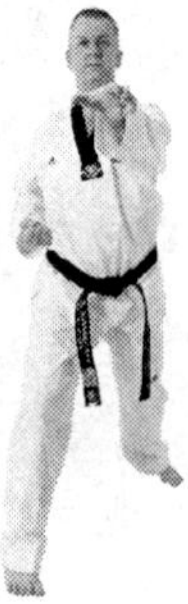

11-1

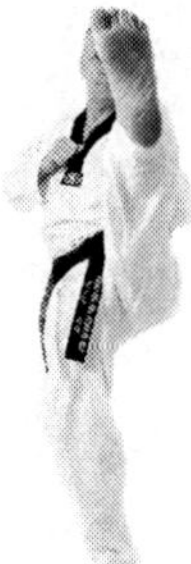

11-2		15		15 Side	

Kihap

11-3		14-2		14-2 Side	

12-1		14-1		14-1 Side	

12-2		13		13 Side	

16 17

18-1 18-2

18-3 18-4

207

208

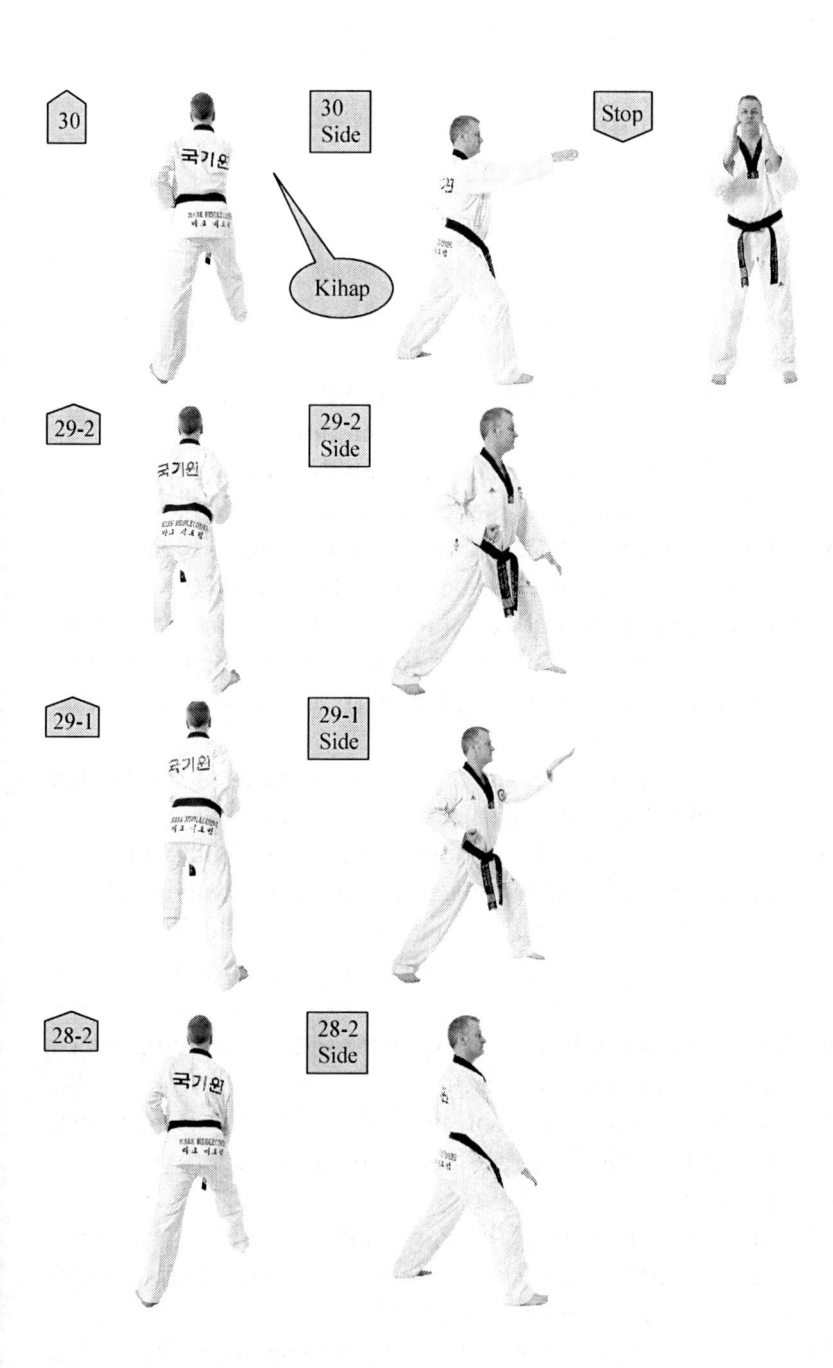

Black Belt Pattern 2 - Keumgang

Poomsae Keumgang - Diamond

Start: Ready stance, facing north.

1. Move forward (move left foot), forward stance, twin outerform block.
2. Move forward, forward stance, palm thrust strike.
3. Move forward, forward stance, palm thrust strike.
4. Move forward, forward stance, palm thrust strike.
5. Move backwards, back stance, inner knife-hand block.
6. Move backwards, back stance, inner knife-hand block.
7. Move backwards, back stance, inner knife-hand block.
8. Move backwards (pull left foot back), crane stance (the body is facing north with the eyes looking west), diamond block (left low block, right high block) performed with force, approximately 8 seconds.
9. Form the right hinge shape (palms facing each other), step down, side horse riding stance, right hook punch.
10. Turn left 360°, side horse riding stance, right hook punch.
11. Turn the body left 90° (move right foot and stamp down with force), side horse riding stance (with the eyes looking north), 'W' block at face height and kihap (left outerform block, right inner block).
12. Turn the body right 180° (move left foot), horse riding stance, twin outerform block (east).
13. Stationary (pull left foot in slightly), ready stance, twin low section block (performed with force, approximately 5 seconds).
14. Turn the body right 180° (move left foot), side horse riding stance (with the eyes looking south), 'W' block at face height (right outerform block, left inner block).
15. Turn the body right 90° (move right foot), crane stance (the

body is facing north with the eyes looking east), diamond block (right low block, left high block) performed with force, approximately 8 seconds.
16. Form the left hinge shape (palms facing each other), step down, side horse riding stance, left hook punch.
17. Turn right 360°, side horse riding stance, left hook punch.
18. Stationary (pull right foot back), crane stance (the body is facing north with the eyes looking east), diamond block (right low block, left high block) performed with force, approximately 8 seconds.
19. Form the left hinge shape (palms facing each other), step down, side horse riding stance, left hook punch.
20. Turn right 360°, side horse riding stance, left hook punch.
21. Turn the body right 90° (move left foot and stamp down with force), side horse riding stance (with the eyes looking north), 'W' block at face height and kihap (right outerform block, left inner block).
22. Turn the body left 180° (move right foot), horse riding stance, twin outerform block (west).
23. Stationary (pull right foot in slightly), ready stance, twin low section block (performed with force, approximately 5 seconds).
24. Turn the body left 180° (move right foot), side horse riding stance (with the eyes looking south), 'W' block at face height (left outerform block, right inner block).
25. Turn the body left 90° (move left foot), crane stance (the body is facing north with the eyes looking west), diamond block (left low block, right high block) performed with force, approximately 8 seconds.
26. Form the right hinge shape (palms facing each other), step down, side horse riding stance, right hook punch.
27. Turn left 360°, side horse riding stance, right hook punch.

End: Form a ready stance. Draw the left foot in slightly and turn the head, facing north.

Notes

Step 2
The right hand is pulled back to the waist when preparing the palm thrust strike to assist power.

Keumgang (27 Steps)

Kihap

214

21

Kihap

22

23

24

25

26

27

Stop

Black Belt Pattern 3 - Taebaek

Poomsae Taebaek - Bright Mountain

Start: Ready stance, facing north.

1. Turn left 90° (move left foot), cat stance, twin low section knife-hand block.
2. Move forward, front kick, forward stance, middle punch, reverse middle punch.
3. Turn right 180° (move right foot), cat stance, twin low section knife-hand block.
4. Move forward, front kick, forward stance, middle punch, reverse middle punch.
5. Turn left 90° (move left foot), forward stance, simultaneous left high knife-hand block and right inner knife-hand strike.
6. Stationary, right palm heel block and grab, move forward, forward stance, reverse middle punch.
7. Stationary, left palm heel block and grab, move forward, forward stance, reverse middle punch.
8. Stationary, right palm heel block and grab, move forward, forward stance, reverse middle punch (kihap).
9. Turn left 270° (move left foot), back stance, twin block (left outerform block, right high block).
10. Stationary, left grab and pull, right uppercut punch (place the left fist on to the right shoulder).
11. Stationary, left punch.
12. Stationary (pull left foot back), crane stance, right hinge shape (left palm facing in).
13. Move forward, simultaneous side kick and side hammer-fist strike, forward stance, reverse horizontal target elbow strike.
14. Turn right 180° (pull the left foot in, feet together, then move the right foot out), back stance, twin block (right outerform block, left high block).

15. Stationary, right grab and pull, left uppercut punch (place the right fist on to the left shoulder).
16. Stationary, right punch.
17. Stationary (pull right foot back), crane stance, left hinge shape (right palm facing in).
18. Move forward, simultaneous side kick and side hammer-fist strike, forward stance, reverse horizontal target elbow strike.
19. Turn left 90° (pull the right foot in, feet together, then move the left foot out), back stance, knife-hand guarding block.
20. Move forward, forward stance, simultaneous left downward palm block, right vertical spear-hand strike.
21. Turn the body left 180° (pivot on the right foot and move the left foot across slightly), forward stance (with the body facing north and the eyes looking over the left shoulder), twist downward right spear-hand, the back of the hand rests at the centre of the small of the back, also position the left knife-hand in front of the solar plexus, palm down. Then turn left 180° (move left foot), back stance, side backfist strike (south).
22. Move forward, forward stance, middle punch (kihap).
23. Turn left 270° (move left foot), forward stance, scissors block (left low block, right outerform block).
24. Move forward, front kick, forward stance, middle punch, reverse middle punch.
25. Turn right 180° (move right foot), forward stance, scissors block (right low block, left outerform block).
26. Move forward, front kick, forward stance, middle punch, reverse middle punch.

End: Form a ready stance. Turn left 90°, pivot on the ball of the right foot and draw the left foot back.

Notes

Steps 1 and 3
The twin low section knife-hand block is positioned just in front of the waist, in line with the thigh of the leading leg.

Taebaek (26 Steps)

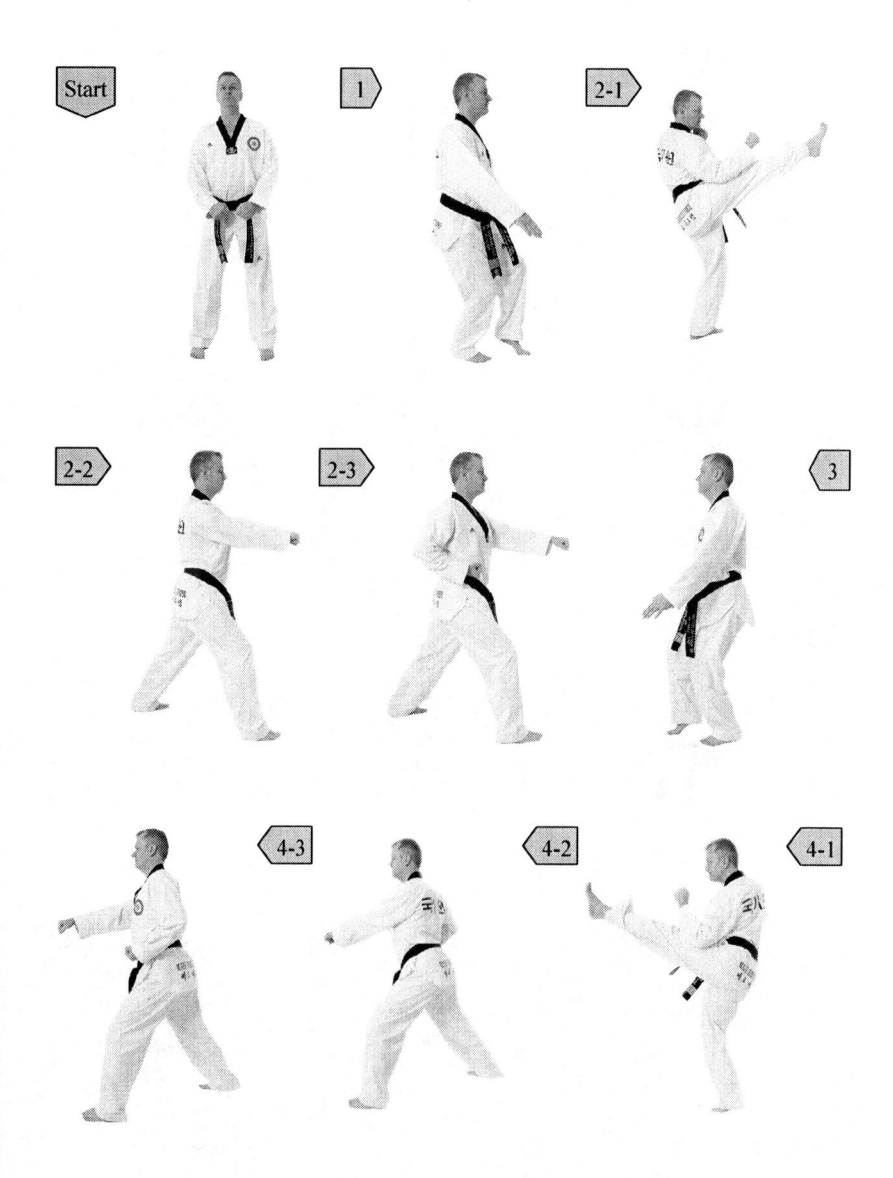

Start | 1 | 2-1

2-2 | 2-3 | 3

4-3 | 4-2 | 4-1

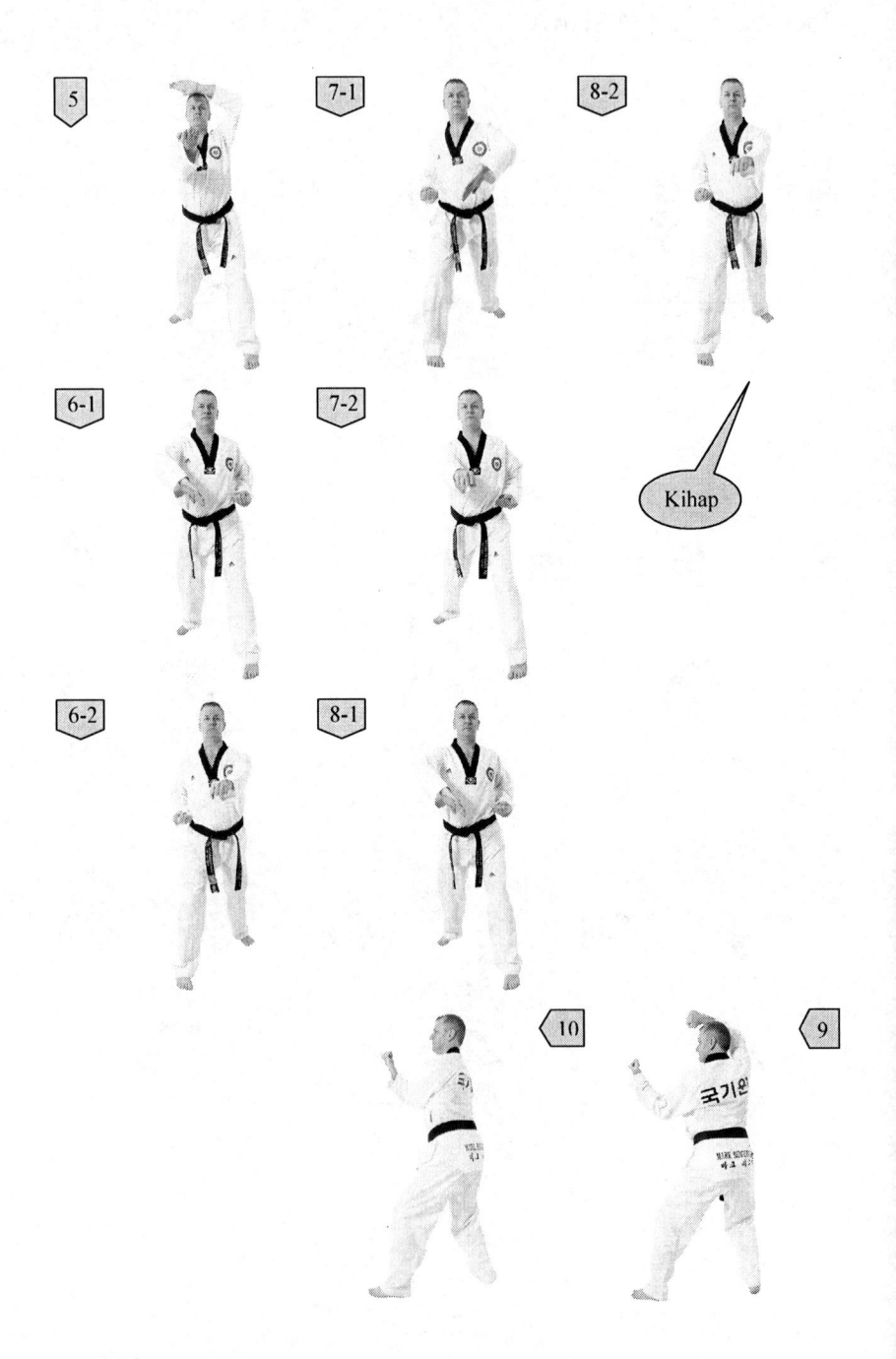

221

223

Black Belt Pattern 4 - Pyongwon

Poomsae Pyongwon - Plain

Start: Close stance, pile of palm, facing north. Palms are positioned facing the lower abdomen with the left hand over the right hand.

1. Move the left leg out to side, ready stance, twin low section knife-hand block (performed in slow motion whilst breathing out).
2. Stationary, raise the hands palms up to the chest, then forwards at neck height, double knife-hand strike with the thumbs tucked in (performed in slow motion, inhale while raising the hands and exhale while pushing outwards).
3. Turn right 90° (move right foot), back stance, low knife-hand block.
4. Turn left 180° (move left foot), back stance, knife-hand block.
5. Stationary, slide left foot forward slightly, forward stance, reverse vertical elbow strike.
6. Move forward, front kick, back kick, land forwards (west) and turn 180° to the right (east), back stance, knife-hand guarding block.
7. Stationary, low knife-hand guarding block.
8. Stationary, move the right foot towards the north direction, side horse riding stance, high section outerform assisted block (simultaneously, position the left fist, with the palm facing down across chest).
9. Stationary, right foot stamp, horse riding stance (north), left fist grab and pull, right front backfist strike and kihap (place the left fist under the right elbow with the palm facing down). Then right fist grab and pull, left front backfist strike (place the right fist under the left elbow with the palm facing down).
10. Turn right 90° (move the left foot in front of the right foot), cross-legged stance, yoke strike.

11. Move forward (move right foot), side horse riding stance, 'W' block (two outerform blocks at face height).
12. Stationary (pull the right foot back), crane stance, diamond block (right low block, left high block). Then form the left hinge shape (the right palm is facing inwards).
13. Move forward, right side kick, forward stance, reverse vertical elbow strike.
14. Move forward, front kick, back kick, landing forwards (east) and turn 180° to the left (west), back stance, knife-hand guarding block.
15. Stationary, low knife-hand guarding block.
16. Stationary, move the left foot towards the north direction, side horse riding stance, high section outerform assisted block (simultaneously, position the right fist, with the palm facing down across chest).
17. Stationary, left foot stamp, horse riding stance (north), right fist grab and pull, left front backfist strike and kihap (place the right fist under the left elbow with the palm facing down). Then left fist grab and pull, right front backfist strike (place the left fist under the right elbow with the palm facing down).
18. Turn left 90° (move the right foot in front of the left foot), cross-legged stance, yoke strike.
19. Move forward (move left foot), side horse riding stance, 'W' block (two outerform blocks at face height).
20. Stationary (pull the left foot back), crane stance, diamond block (left low block, right high block). Then form the right hinge shape (the left palm is facing inwards).
21. Move forward, simultaneous left side kick and left side hammer-fist strike, forward stance, reverse horizontal target elbow strike.

End: Form a close stance, pile of palm. Turn right 90°, pivot on the ball of the right foot and draw the left foot back.

Notes

Steps 5 and 13
The vertical elbow strike must be executed at chin height.

Steps 6 and 14
After the front kick has been executed, step down with the foot turned to assist a smooth transition for the back kick.

Steps 7 and 15
Perform the low section knife-hand guarding block with a large circular action over the head.

Steps 9 and 17
The front backfist strike must be set up behind the head, above the shoulder.

Notes

Pyongwon   (21 Steps)

Start

1

2

3

4

5

6-1

6-2

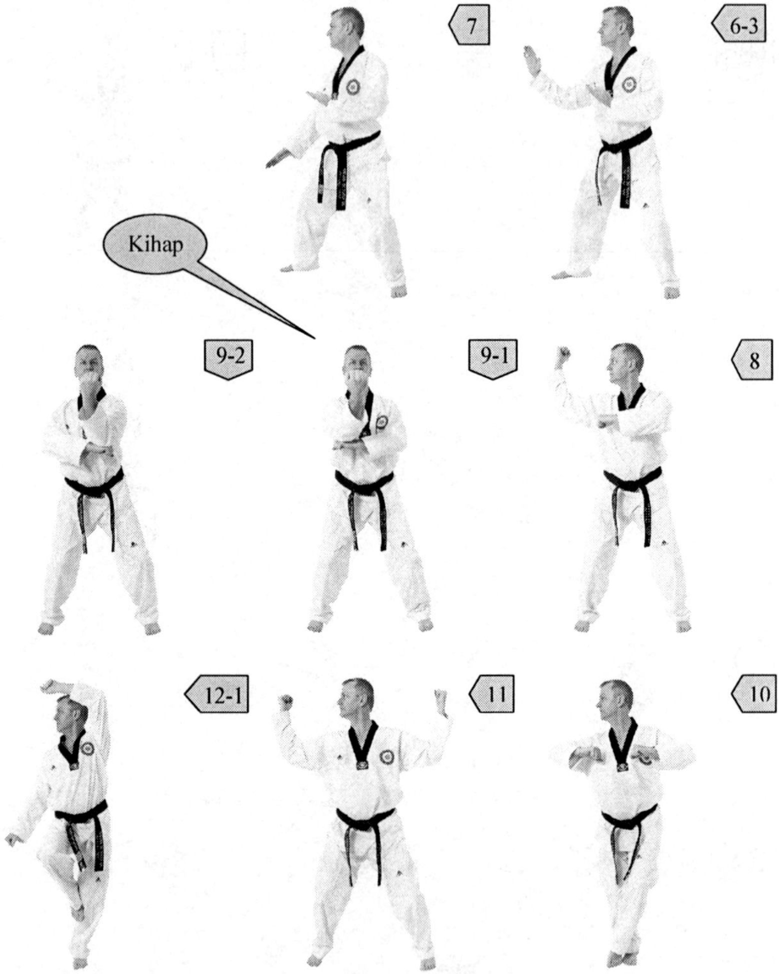
7
6-3
Kihap
9-2
9-1
8
12-1
11
10

12-2

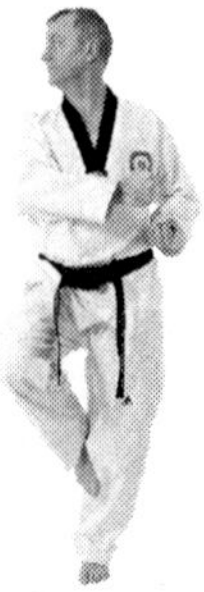

13-1

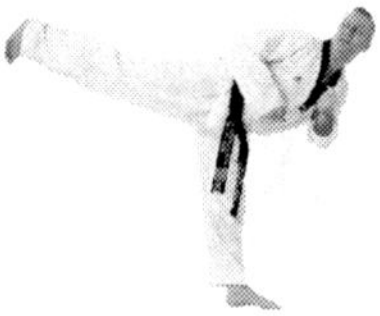

13-2

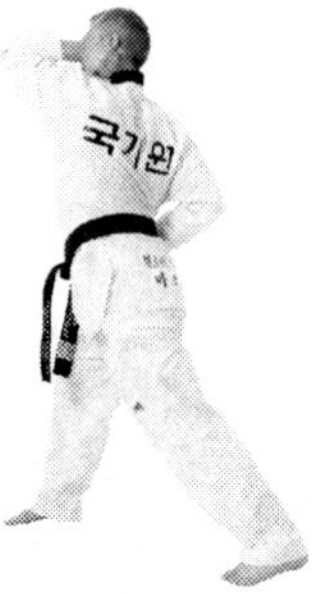

14-1

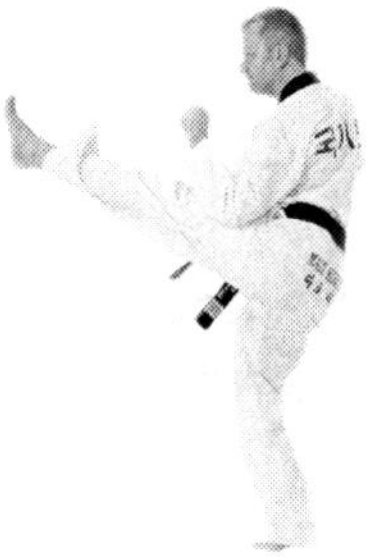

14-2

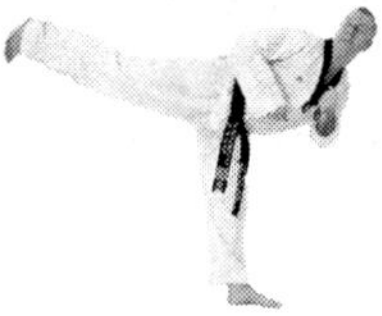

14-3

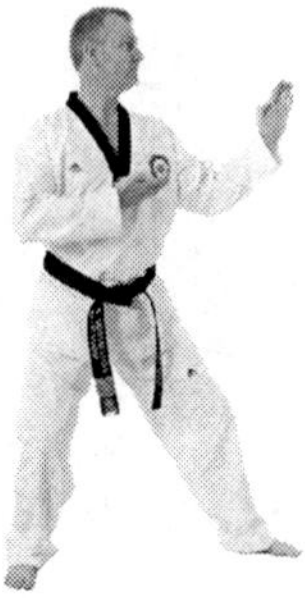

15

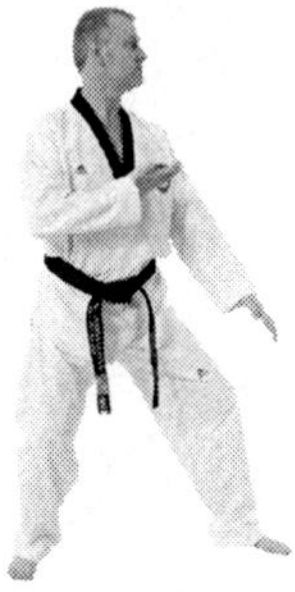

16

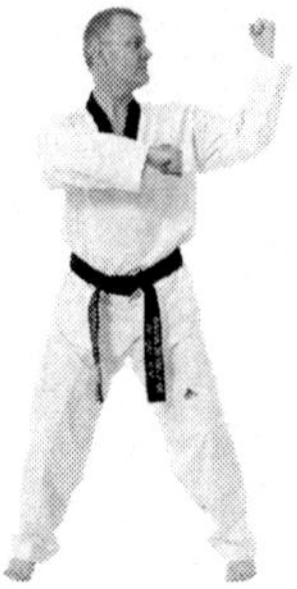

| 17-1 | 17-2 | 18 |

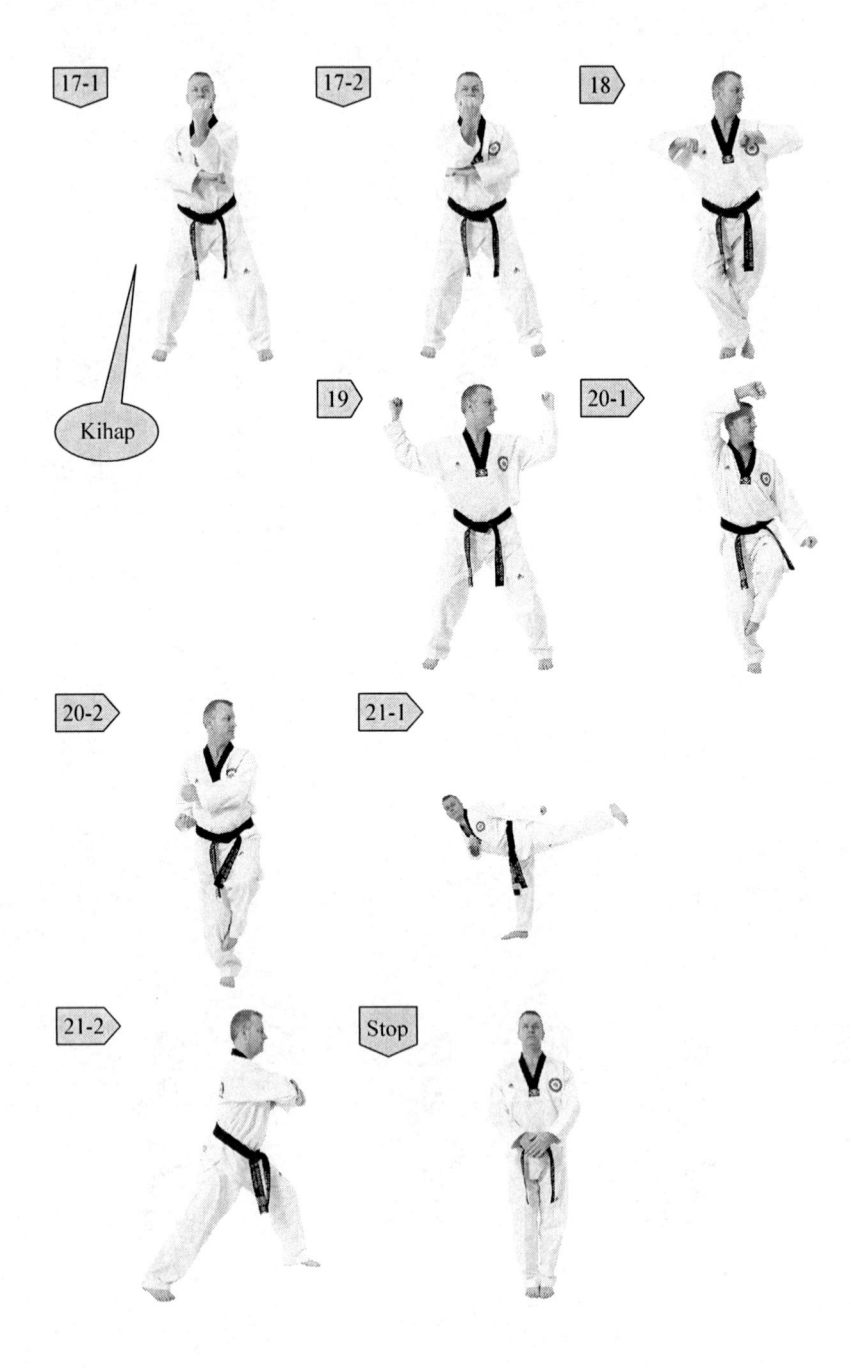

Kihap

| 19 | 20-1 |

| 20-2 | 21-1 |

| 21-2 | Stop |

232

Black Belt Pattern 5 - Sipjin

Poomsae Sipjin - Decimal

Start: Ready stance, facing north.

1. Stationary, raise forearms together to chest height (performed in slow motion), then snap outwards, bull block (the fists are one fist distance apart). Then pull fists down slightly (so that the fists are two fist distance apart).
2. Turn left 90° (move left foot), back stance, hand supported outerform block.
3. Stationary, slowly with force, turn the left fist inward and open the hand, as soon as the hand is open and the palm is facing down, simultaneously slide the left foot forward, forward stance, and execute a reverse spear-hand strike (palm down). Then punch, reverse punch.
4. Move forward, side horse riding stance, 'W' block.
5. Move forward (move the left foot in front of the right foot), cross-legged stance, and reach out with the left hand to grab the opponent's lapel, then move the right foot out, side horse riding stance, side punch (kihap).
6. Turn left 180° (move right foot), side horse riding stance, yoke strike.
7. Move forward (move the left foot in), close stance, then move the right foot out, back stance, hand supported outerform block.
8. Stationary, slowly with force, turn the right fist inward and open the hand, as soon as the hand is open and the palm is facing down, simultaneously slide the right foot forward, forward stance, and execute a reverse spear-hand strike (palm down). Then punch, reverse punch.
9. Move forward, side horse riding stance, 'W' block.
10. Move forward (move the right foot in front of the left foot),

cross-legged stance, and reach out with the right hand to grab the opponent's lapel, then move the left foot out, side horse riding stance, side punch (kihap).
11. Turn right 180° (move left foot), side horse riding stance, yoke strike (with the body facing north and the eyes looking west).
12. Turn right 270° (move right foot, the left foot pivots 90° to the right), back stance, hand supported outerform block (south).
13. Stationary, slowly with force, turn the right fist inward and open the hand, as soon as the hand is open and the palm is facing down, simultaneously slide the right foot forward, forward stance, and execute a reverse spear-hand strike (palm down). Then punch, reverse punch.
14. Move forward, back stance, low knife-hand guarding block.
15. Move forward, forward stance, boulder pushing (performed with force).
16. Turn left 90° (move right foot), horse riding stance, twin knife-hand outerform block.
17. Stationary, twin low knife-hand block (in slow motion).
18. Stationary, when step 17 is almost completed, simultaneously clench the fists powerfully and straighten the legs (in slow motion), twin low block.
19. Turn left 90° (move left foot), forward stance, pull lift block (the left arm is placed in front of the chest with the palm facing inwards).
20. Stationary, boulder pushing (performed with force).
21. Move forward, simultaneous front kick and pull the arms to the left side of the waist (small hinge shape), forward stance, two-fisted punch.
22. Move forward, simultaneous front kick and pull the arms to the right side of the waist (small hinge shape), forward stance, two-fisted punch.
23. Move forward, simultaneous front kick and pull the arms to the left side of the waist (small hinge shape), cross-legged stance, assisted front backfist strike and kihap (the left fist is placed in front of the solar plexus with the palm facing up).
24. Turn left 180° (move left foot), forward stance, boulder

pushing (performed with force).
25. Stationary, pull left foot back slightly, cat stance, twin low knife-hand 'X' block (the palms are facing outward).
26. Move forward, back stance, right assisted ridge-hand block, (the left knife-hand is placed in front of the solar plexus with the palm facing down).
27. Move forward, back stance, two-fisted punch.
28. Move forward, back stance, two-fisted punch.

End: Form a ready stance. Turn left 180°, pivot on the ball of the left foot and draw the right foot back.

_____ Notes _____

Steps 21, 22, 27 and 28
The reverse punch must be placed at the middle of the forearm with a gap of two fists distance and with the elbow slightly bent.

Steps 27 and 28
The two-fisted punch must be set up by making a small hinge shape at the reverse side of the waist.

Notes

Sipjin (28 Steps)

Start	1-1	1-2
2	3-1	3-2
3-3	4	5-1

Kihap

11

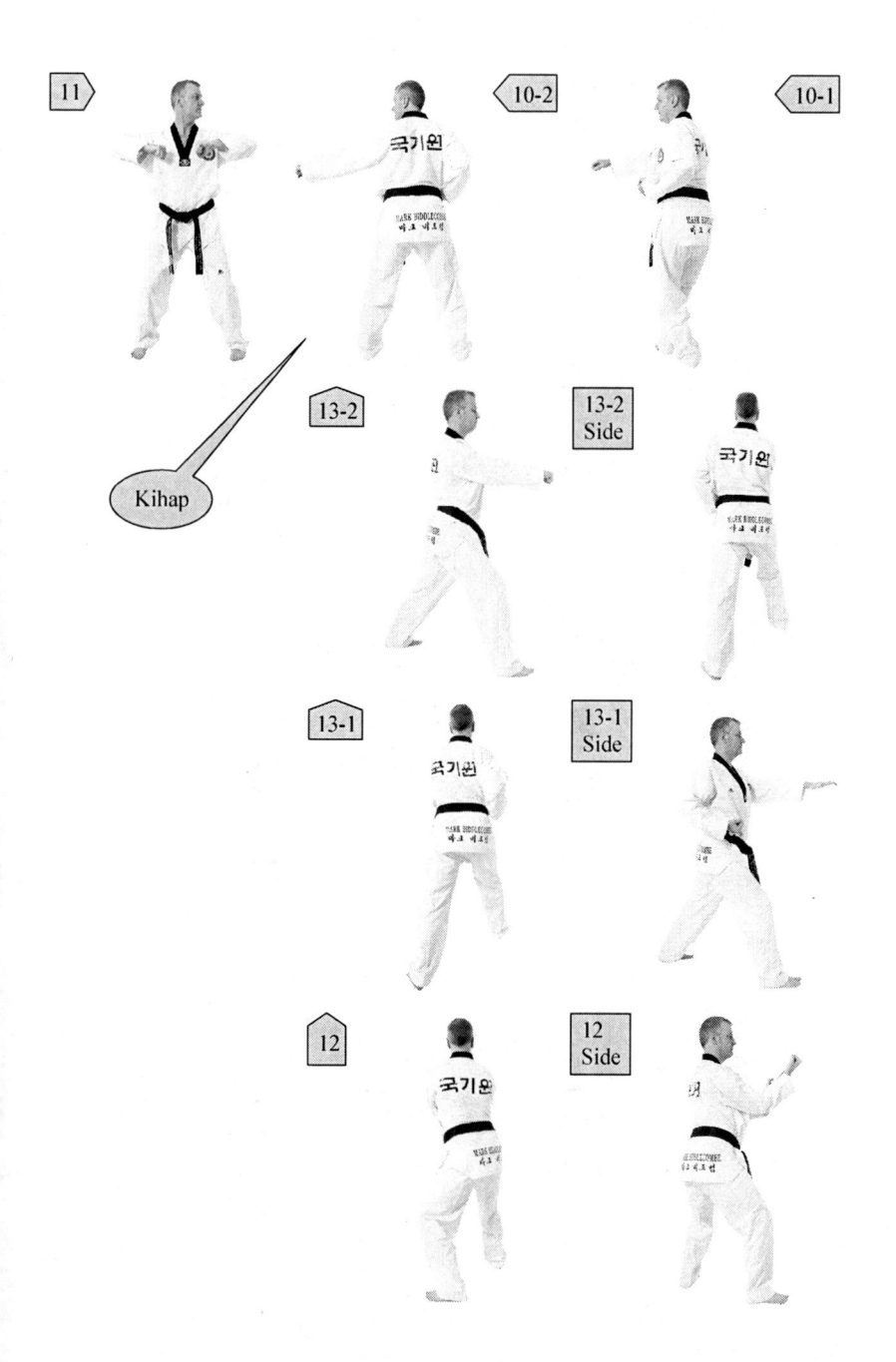

10-2

10-1

Kihap

13-2

13-2 Side

13-1

13-1 Side

12

12 Side

239

15-2

15-2 Side

15-1

15-1 Side

14

14 Side

13-3

13-3 Side

Kihap

26-1
Set up

25-2

25-2
Side

25-1
Set up

24

24
Side

| 28 | 28 Side | Stop |

| 27-2 | 27-2 Side |

| 27-1 Set up |

| 26-2 | 26-2 Side |

Black Belt Pattern 6 - Jitae

Poomsae Jitae - Earth

Start: Ready stance, facing north.

1. Turn left 90° (move left foot), back stance, outerform block.
2. Move forward, forward stance, high block, reverse middle punch (both actions must be performed with force, approximately 8 seconds apiece).
3. Turn right 180° (move right foot), back stance, outerform block.
4. Move forward, forward stance, high block, reverse middle punch (both actions must be performed with force, approximately 8 seconds apiece).
5. Turn left 90° (move left foot), forward stance, low block.
6. Stationary, pull front leg back slightly, back stance, high knife-hand block.
7. Move forward, front kick, back stance, low knife-hand guarding block.
8. Stationary, reverse outerform block (right hand, performed with force).
9. Move forward, front kick, back stance, low knife-hand guarding block.
10. Stationary, slide front leg forward slightly, forward stance, high block (performed with force).
11. Move forward, forward stance, diamond punch (simultaneous middle punch, reverse high block).
12. Stationary, reverse inner block, then keeping the reverse inner block in place, swiftly using the other arm, inner block (both arms acting like a scissors block).
13. Move backwards, back stance, low knife-hand block.
14. Stationary, front kick (replace the kicking foot behind), forward stance, reverse punch, punch.

15. Move backwards, turn left 90° (move left foot), horse riding stance, bull block.
16. Stationary, turn the head left 90°, facing south, side horse riding stance, left low block.
17. Stationary, turn the head right 180°, facing north, side horse riding stance, right knife-hand block.
18. Stationary, left hammer-fist target strike and kihap. The right palm is turned so that the fingers are horizontal to the floor at face height.
19. Stationary, pull right foot back, crane stance, right low block.
20. Stationary, form the left hinge shape (right palm facing in).
21. Stationary, side kick, replace the left foot with the right foot and turn the head left 180°, facing south, crane stance, left low block.
22. Stationary, form the right hinge shape (left palm facing in).
23. Stationary, side kick, land the kicking foot moving forward (south), forward stance, reverse punch.
24. Move forward, forward stance, punch and kihap.
25. Turn left 270° (move left foot), back stance, low knife-hand guarding block.
26. Move forward, back stance, knife-hand guarding block.
27. Turn right 180° (move right foot), back stance, low knife-hand guarding block.
28. Move forward, back stance, knife-hand guarding block.

End: Form a ready stance. Turn left 90°, pivot on the ball of the right foot and pull the left foot back.

Notes

Steps 5 and 6
The actions must be performed swiftly and continuously.

Steps 19-24
The actions must be performed continuously as a rapid sequence.

Jitae   (28 Steps)

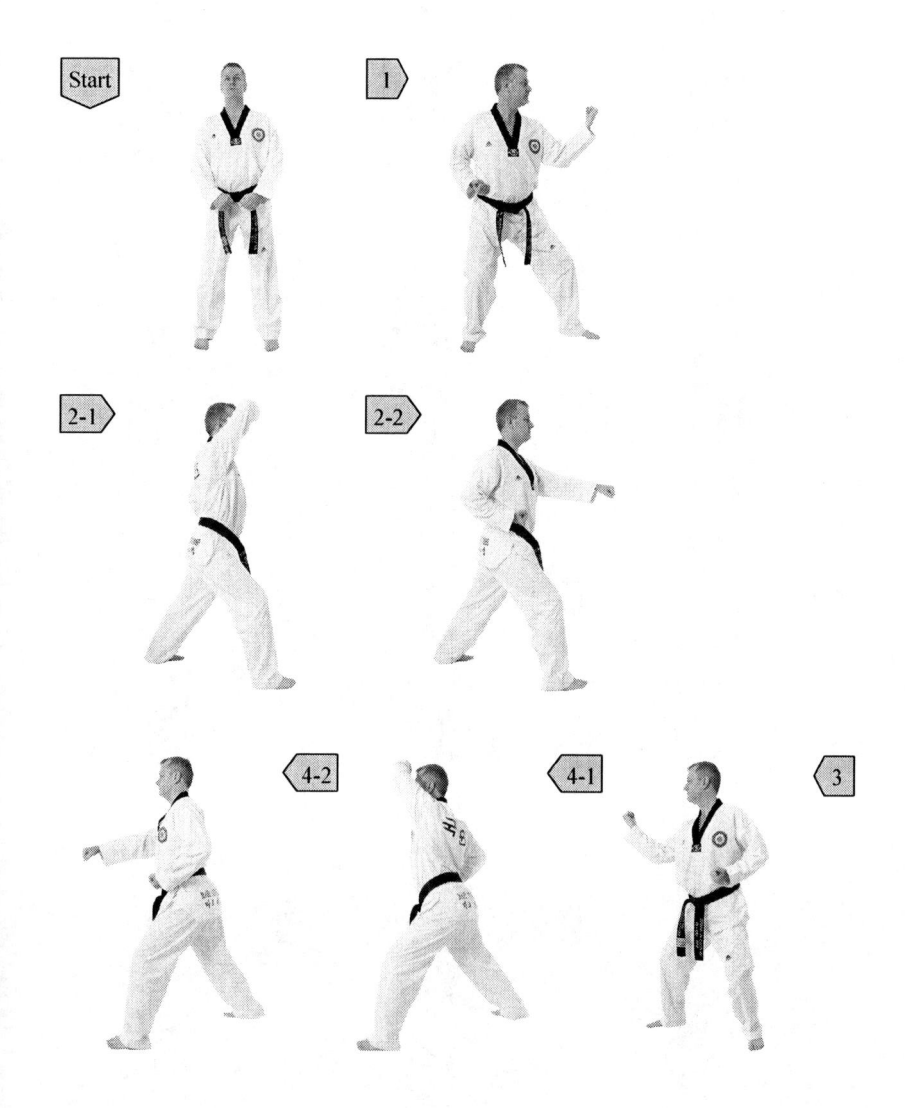

5

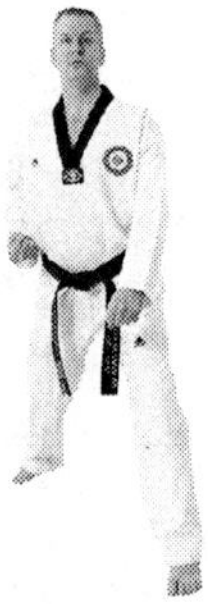

6

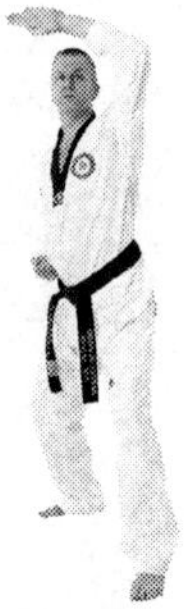

7-1

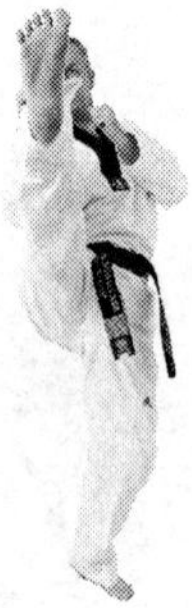

7-2

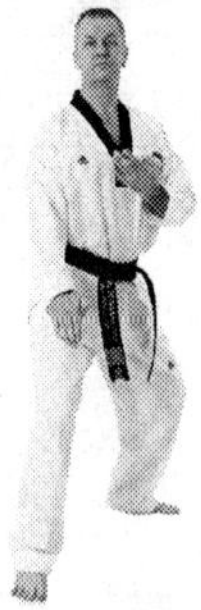

8

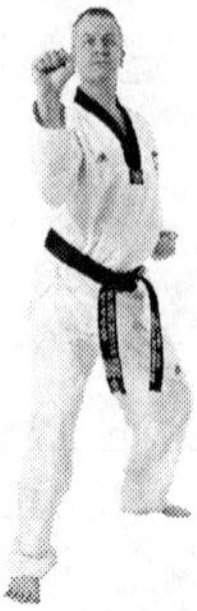

9-1

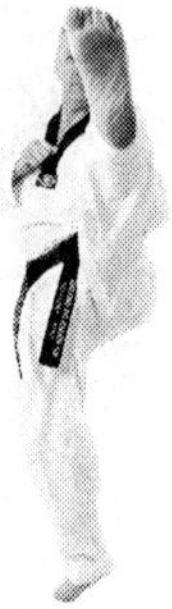

9-2

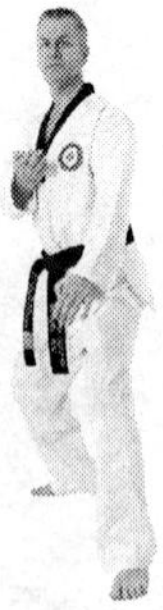

10

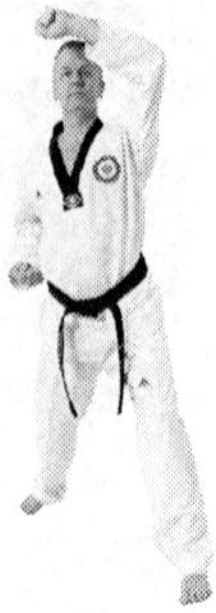

11-1

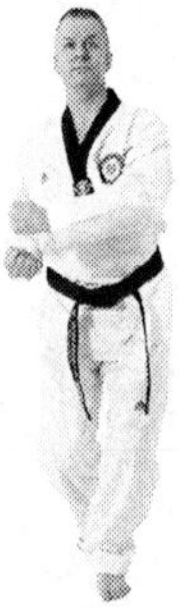

11-2

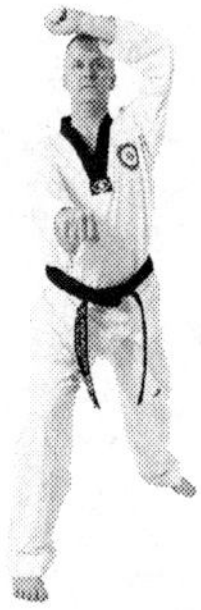

12-1

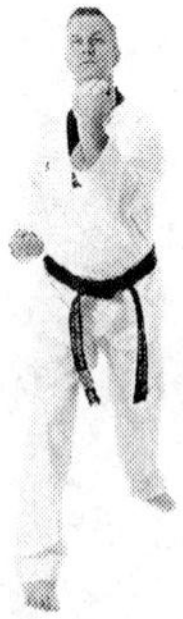

12-2

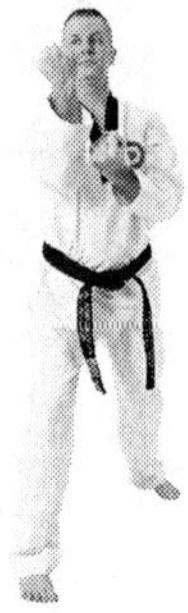

14-3

18

Kihap

14-2

17

14-1

16

16
Side

13

15

249

19

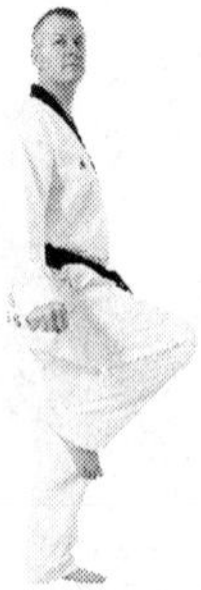

19
Side

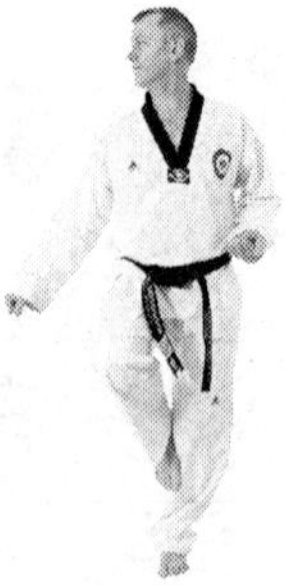

20

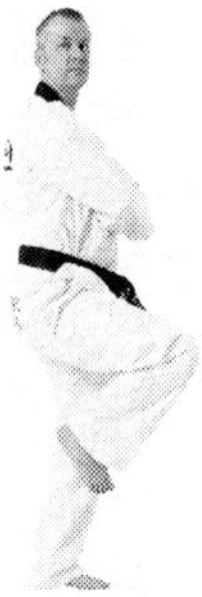

20
Side

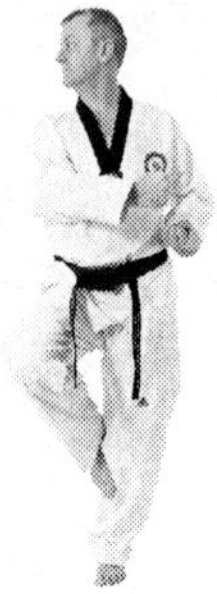

23-1

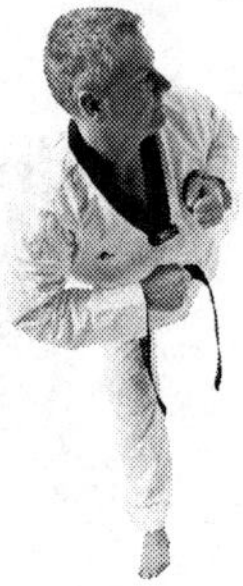

21-1

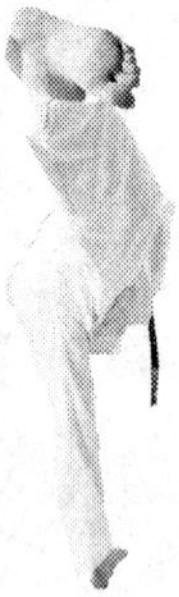

22

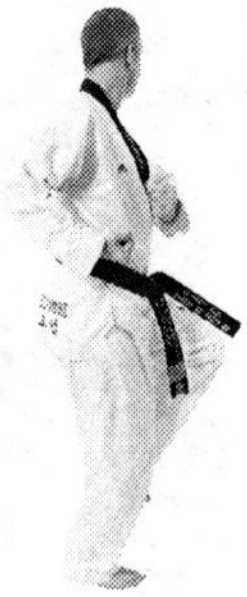

21-2
Side

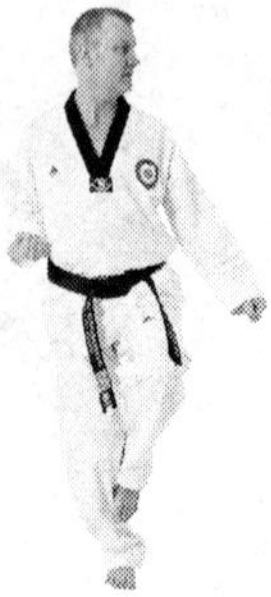

21-2

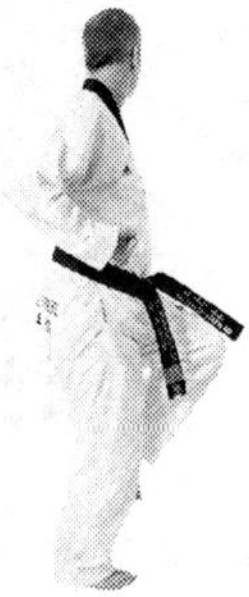

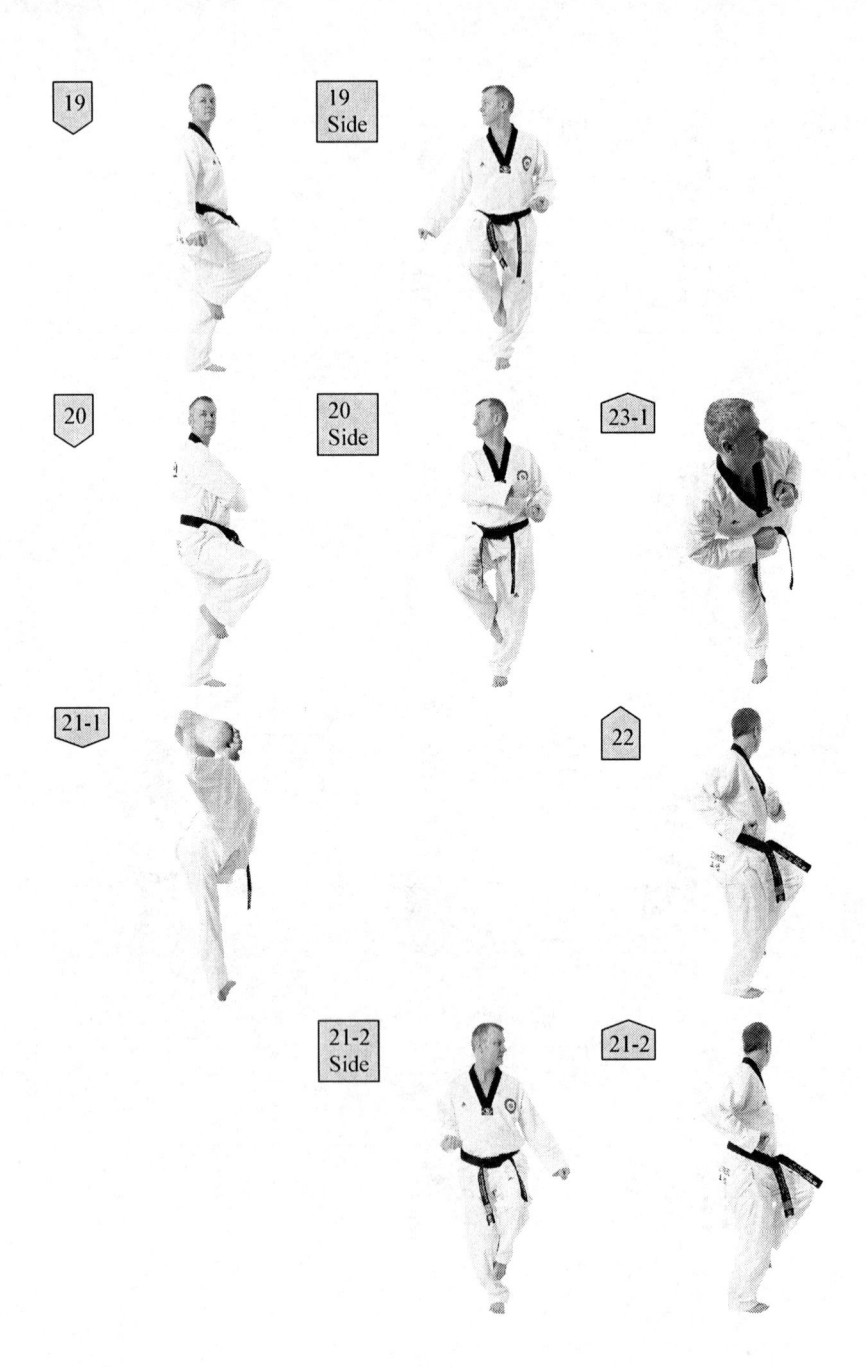

24 Kihap

24 Side

23-2

23-2 Side

25

26

Stop

28

27

251

Black Belt Pattern 7 - Chonkwon

Poomsae Chonkwon - Sky

Start: Close stance, pile of palm.

1. Stationary, move the hands up in front of the chest (inhale while performing the action, the palms face inwards), then spread of wings (exhale and perform with force).
2. Stationary, knife-hand bull block, and then move backwards (move left foot), cat stance, twin middle knuckle uppercut punch.
3. Move right foot forward slightly, forward stance, reverse knife-hand block.
4. Stationary, with the left hand grab and pull the opponent's wrist, then move forward, forward stance, reverse punch (performed with force, approximately 8 seconds).
5. Stationary, forward stance, reverse knife-hand block.
6. Stationary, with the right hand grab and pull the opponent's wrist, then move forward, forward stance, reverse punch (performed with force, approximately 8 seconds).
7. Stationary, forward stance, reverse knife-hand block.
8. Stationary, grab and twist the opponent's wrist, then move forward, simultaneously pull the opponent's wrist and execute a side kick (kihap), forward stance, low block.
9. Move forward, forward stance, punch.
10. Turn left 270°, move left foot, back stance, outerform guarding block.
11. Stationary, circular action high block and side punch (the right fist is placed at the side of the waist).
12. Move forward, left high knife-hand block (catch and pull the opponent's wrist), back stance, right side punch.
13. Turn right 180°, move right foot, back stance, outerform guarding block.

14. Stationary, circular action high block and side punch (the left fist is placed at the side of the waist).
15. Move forward, right high knife-hand block (catch and pull the opponent's wrist), back stance, left side punch.
16. Turn left 90° (move left foot), forward stance, outerform block with the right hand.
17. Stationary, punch.
18. Move forward, front kick, forward stance, punch.
19. Stationary, pull right foot back slightly, back stance, low knife-hand guarding block.
20. Trotting forward, make sure the body weight is over the left foot and move the right foot forward slightly, then draw the left foot up close behind the right foot, assisted outerform block (the left palm is turned down and is struck by the right forearm as it is raised for the outerform block). Move the right foot forward again, back stance, low guarding block (the left palm is turned up and is struck by the right forearm as it is lowered for the low guarding block).
21. Stationary, move right foot across slightly, side horse riding stance, diamond side punch (with the body facing east and the eyes looking south).
22. Move forward, 360° jumping inner crescent target kick, side horse riding stance, diamond side punch.
23. Turn left 180° (move the left foot outward slightly), back stance (north), half mountain knife-hand block (performed in slow motion with controlled breathing).
24. Turn right 180° (pivot on the heels of the feet), back stance (south), half mountain knife-hand block (performed in slow motion with controlled breathing).
25. Turn left 180° (pull the left foot back), close stance, pile of palm. Raise the hands in a large circular action above the head (in the shape of a knife-hand bull block) and then back down to the sides of the waist. Slide the right foot forward, cat stance, push mountain, performed with force, approximately 5 seconds (the right hand is placed at the abdomen, and the left hand is placed just below eye level).

26. Stationary, pull right foot back, close stance, pile of palm, raise the hands in a large circular action above the head (in the shape of a knife-hand bull block) and then back down to the sides of the waist. Slide the left foot forward, cat stance, push mountain, performed with force, approximately 5 seconds (the left hand is placed at the abdomen, and the right hand is placed just below eye level).

End: Form a close stance, pile of palm. Pull the left foot back.

Notes

Step 2
The bull knife-hand block must be performed with a large circular action.

Steps 11 and 12 and 14 and 15
The movements must be performed in one continuous sequence.

Step 21
The diamond side punch must be set up at the right side of the waist by forming a small hinge shape.

Steps 25 and 26
The arm for the palm strike to the chin is straightened. The arm for the palm strike to the abdomen is slightly bent at the elbow.

Notes

Chonkwon (26 Steps)

Start

1-1

1-2

2-1

2-2

3

4

5

6

7

8-1

Kihap

13-1	13-2
14-1	14-2
15-1	15-2
16	16 Side

19	19 Side
18-2	18-2 Side
18-1	18-1 Side
17	17 Side

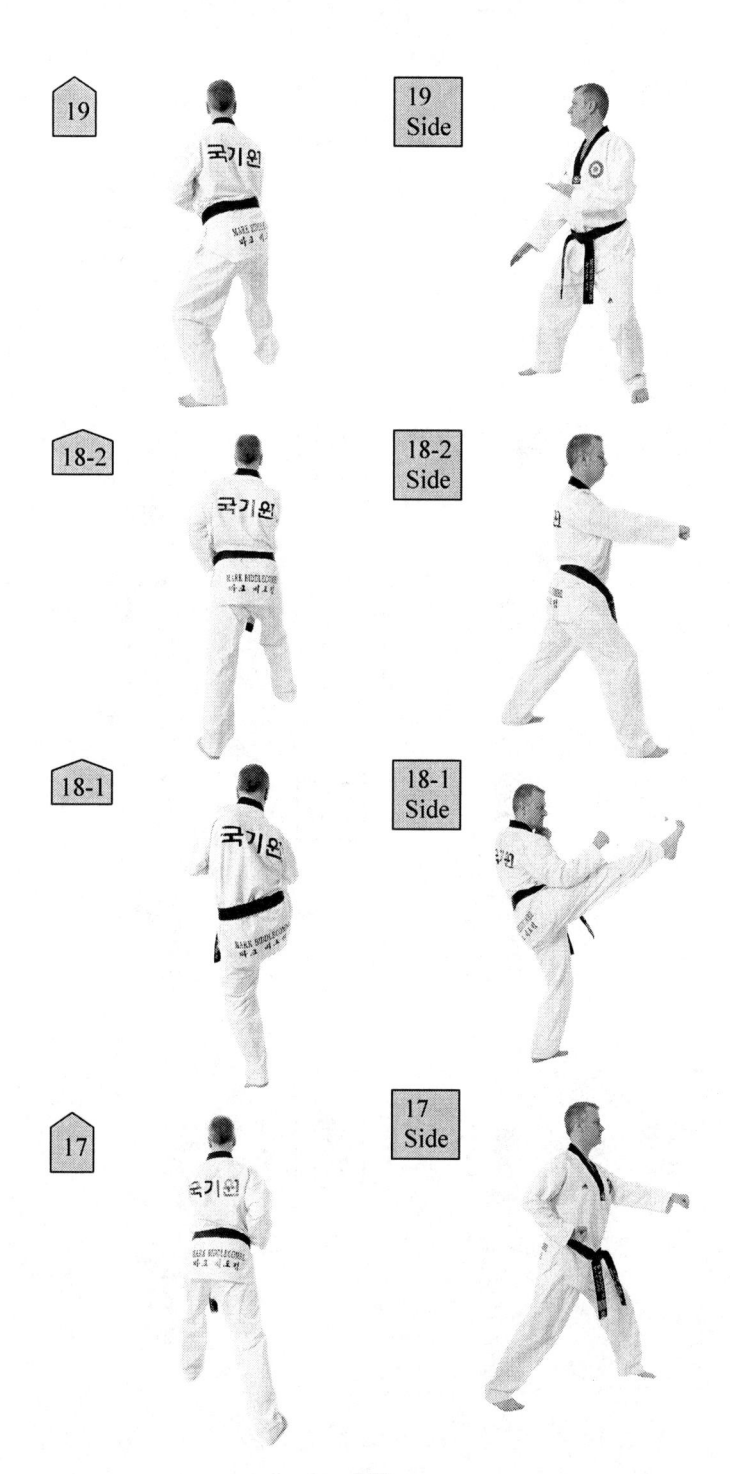

22-1

22-1 Side

21

21 Side

20-2

20-2 Side

20-1

20-1 Side

24

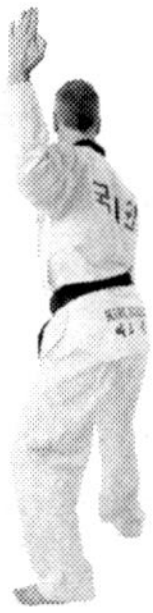

25-1

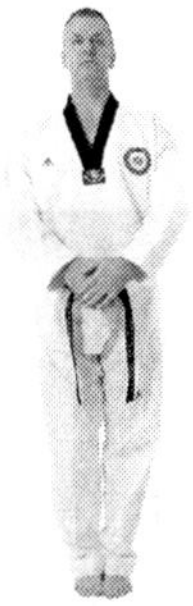

26-2

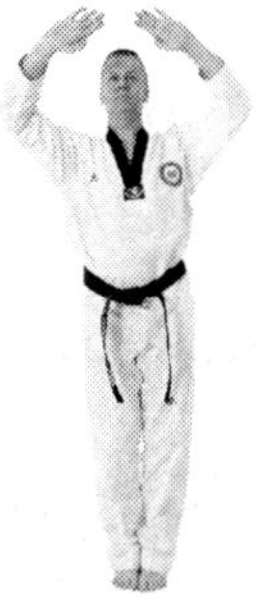

23

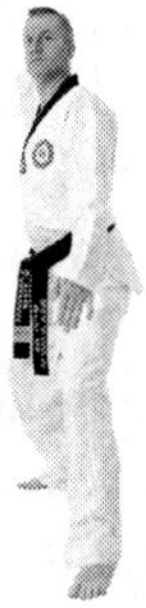

25-2

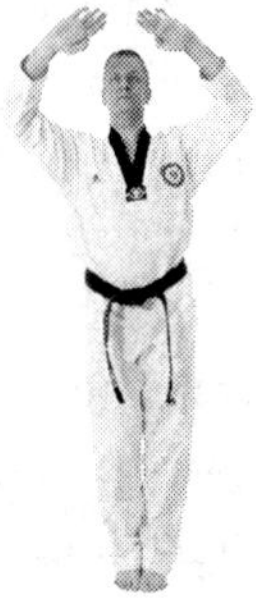

26-3

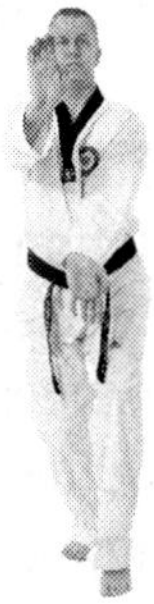

22-2
Side

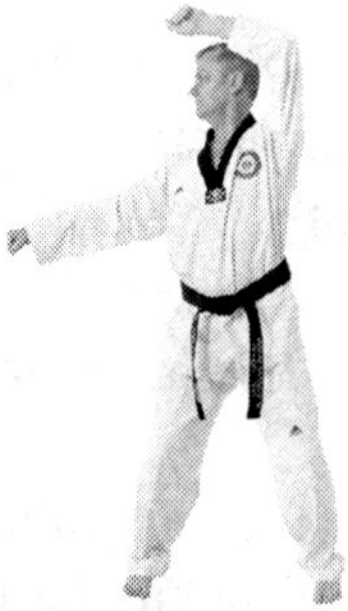

25-3

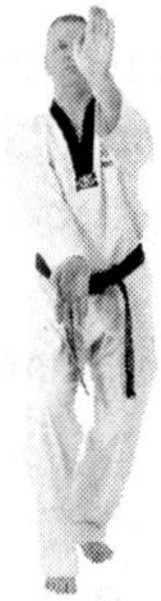

22-2

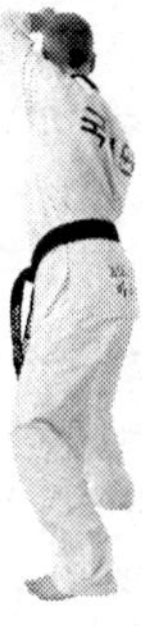

26-1

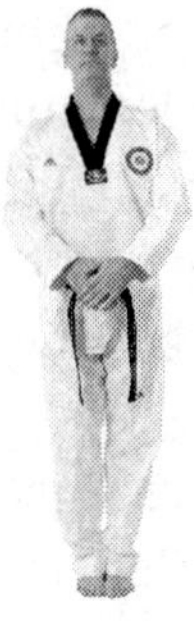

Stop

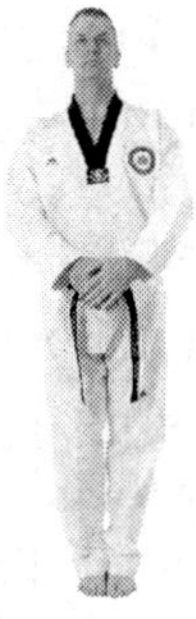

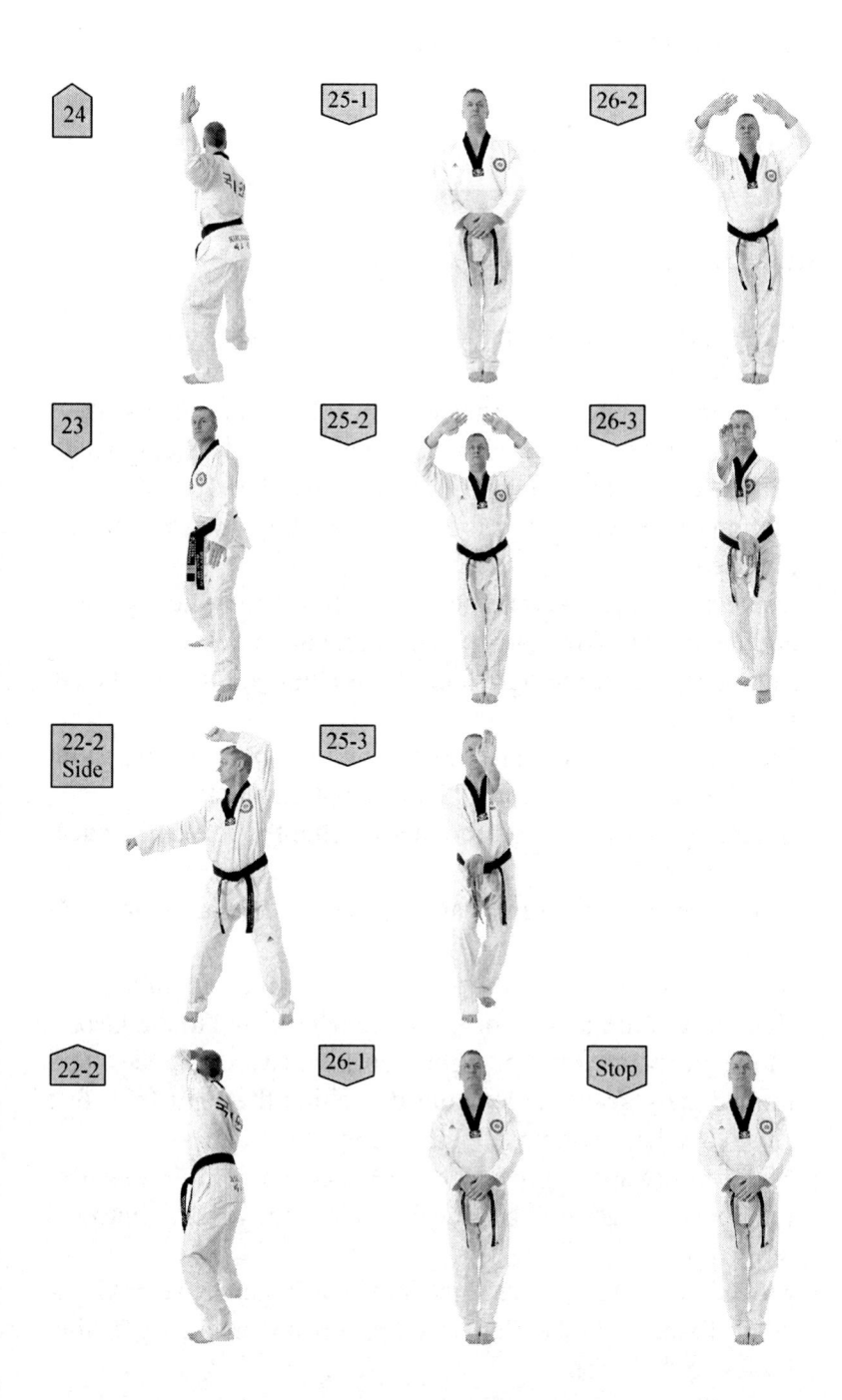

Black Belt Pattern 8 - Hansu

Poomsae Hansu - Water

Start: Close stance, pile of palm.

1. Move forward (move left foot), forward stance, twin outerform ridge hand block.
2. Move forward, forward stance, twin side hammer-fist strike.
3. Move backward, forward stance (with the body facing south and the eyes looking north), half mountain block.
4. Stationary, move the left foot across slightly, forward stance, reverse punch.
5. Move backward, forward stance (with the body facing south and the eyes looking north), half mountain block.
6. Stationary, move the right foot across slightly, forward stance, reverse punch.
7. Move backward, forward stance (with the body facing south and the eyes looking north), half mountain block.
8. Stationary, move the left foot across slightly, forward stance, reverse punch.
9. Move forward, forward stance, twin outerform ridge hand block.
10. Move forward 45° (northwest), forward stance, simultaneous right downward palm block, left arc hand strike to the throat.
11. Move forward (move right foot), forward stance, and immediately draw the left foot up behind the right foot, feet close together, twin upset punch to the abdomen.
12. Move backwards (move left foot), side horse riding stance, inner wrist target low block, place the right wrist up into the left palm.
13. Move backwards (move right foot), back stance, twin knife-hand diamond block (left low knife-hand block, right high knife-hand block).

14. Stationary, pull the left foot back, crane stance, turn the head left 90° (looking southwest), right hinge shape (left palm facing in).
15. Move forward, side kick (southwest), forward stance, simultaneous left high knife-hand block, right inner knife-hand strike.
16. Move forward, front kick, cross-legged stance (stamp down), front backfist strike and kihap.
17. Turn left 180° (move left foot out, looking northeast), side horse riding stance, outer knife-hand strike.
18. Move forward, inner crescent target kick (northeast), side horse riding stance, right horizontal target elbow strike.
19. Move forward (move left foot), close stance. Then move forward again (move right foot), forward stance, simultaneous left downward palm block, right arc hand strike to the throat.
20. Move forward (move left foot), forward stance, and immediately draw the right foot up behind the left foot, feet close together, twin upset punch to the abdomen.
21. Move backwards (move right foot), side horse riding stance, inner wrist target low block, place the left wrist up into the right palm.
22. Move backwards (move left foot), back stance, twin knife-hand diamond block (right low knife-hand block, left high knife-hand block).
23. Stationary, pull the right foot back, crane stance, turn the head right 90° (looking southeast), left hinge shape (right palm facing in).
24. Move forward, side kick (southeast), forward stance, simultaneous right high knife-hand block, left inner knife-hand strike.
25. Move forward, front kick, cross-legged stance (stamp down), front backfist strike and kihap.
26. Turn right 180° (move right foot out, looking northwest), side horse riding stance, outer knife-hand strike.
27. Move forward, inner crescent target kick (northwest), side horse riding stance, left horizontal target elbow strike.

End: Form a close stance, pile of palm (facing north). Pull right foot back.

Notes

Steps 3, 5 and 7
The feet are placed at an angle of 45° (this is the same as the forward stances in steps 5 and 7 of Taegeuk pattern 8).

Steps 12 and 21
The four fingers rest on the back of the hand with the thumb against the inside of the wrist.

Notes

Hansu (27 Steps)

Start

1

2

3

3 Side

4

5

6

7

8

9

267

Kihap

15-2
16-1
16-2
17
18-1
18-2
19

269

Black Belt Pattern 9 - Ilyeo

Poomsae Ilyeo - Oneness

Start: Close stance, covering fist.

1. Move forward (move left foot), back stance, knife-hand guarding block.
2. Move forward, forward stance, punch.
3. Turn left 90° (move left foot up), back stance, diamond block (performed with force).
4. Turn left 90° (move left foot across), back stance, knife-hand guarding block.
5. Stationary, reverse punch.
6. Move forward (move right foot), crane stance (the left foot is placed behind the right knee), simultaneous left vertical spear-hand strike, right downward palm block (south) and kihap.
7. Stationary, simultaneous left side kick (south), half mountain block (right outerform block, left low block). Performed with force.
8. Move forward (step down with the left foot), back stance, high 'X' block.
9. Move forward, grab and pull the opponent's wrist, forward stance and punch.
10. Turn left 90° (move left foot up), back stance, diamond block (performed with force).
11. Turn left 90° (move left foot across), back stance, knife-hand guarding block.
12. Stationary, reverse punch.
13. Move forward (move right foot), crane stance (the left foot is placed behind the right knee), simultaneous right vertical spear-hand strike, left downward palm block (north) and kihap.
14. Turn left 90°, simultaneous left side kick (west), half mountain

block (right outerform block, left low block). Performed with force.
15. Move forward (step down with the left foot), back stance (west), high 'X' block.
16. Move forward, grab and pull the opponent's wrist, forward stance and punch.
17. Turn left 90° (move left foot up), back stance (south), diamond block (performed with force).
18. Turn left 90° (move left foot), close stance (east), place the fists at the side of the waist.
19. Move forward, right front kick (land in front and spring up), left flying side kick, back stance, high 'X' block.
20. Move forward, grab and pull the opponent's wrist, forward stance and punch.
21. Turn left 90° (move left foot up), back stance (north), diamond block (performed with force).
22. Turn left 90° (move left foot), close stance (west), place the fists at the side of the waist.
23. Move forward, left front kick (land in front and spring up), right flying side kick, back stance, high 'X' block.

End: Form a close stance, covering fist. Turn right 90°, pivot on the ball of the left foot and draw the right foot back.

Notes

Ready stance
The covering fist is placed at the height of the philtrum (this is the same as step 11 of Taegeuk pattern 7).

Ilyeo (23 Steps)

Start

1
2
3
4
5
6
7

4 Side
5 Side
6 Side
7 Side

Kihap

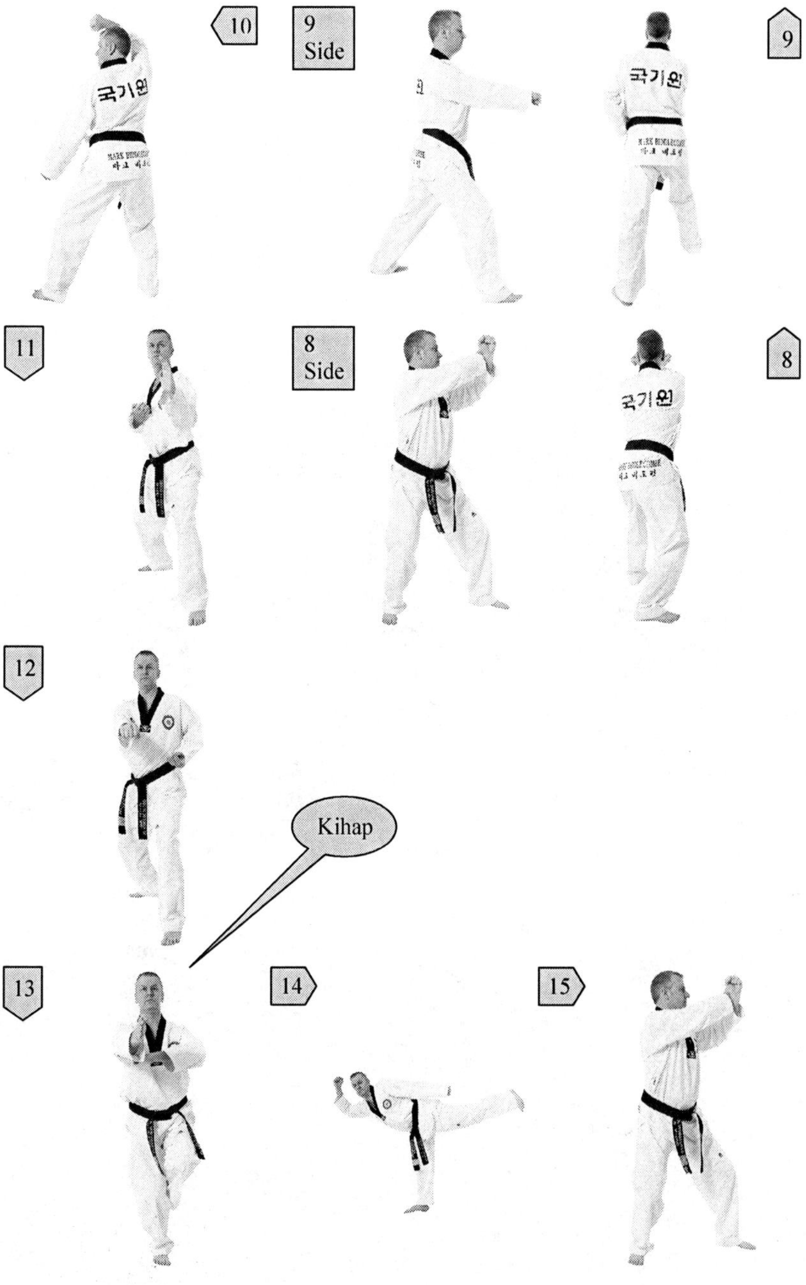
10
9
Side
9
11
8
Side
8
12
Kihap
13
14
15

21

22

23-1

23-2

23-3

Stop

Reflection

I have been asked how I approach patterns and I usually reply, "I try to do each move perfectly". I have had to commit time, effort and hard work in order to achieve each goal. I have not given myself the luxury of accepting a 'near enough goals' approach. I have needed to be disciplined and determined, setting achievable targets. With this approach I have found that my performances and my confidence have become stronger. I have always adhered to the principle that my ultimate competition is with myself. I have never relaxed this approach. Even when training for my 7th Dan, I disciplined myself to developing my skills and performance. Having made this commitment, I presented in Korea in front of the panel, prepared. I was contented with the progress I had made and was confident. I achieved my goal. This approach has served me well throughout my career in Taekwondo. I am never satisfied that I have 'arrived'. Training and development continue because there is always more to learn. See my website: www.theheartoftaekwondo.com.

Final word

The Heart of Taekwondo

Perfect Patterns   Achieve Power   Earn Promotion

I hope you have enjoyed reading The Heart of Taekwondo as much as I have writing it. I hope this book will assist all practitioners in the understanding and development of Taekwondo techniques, philosophy and principles. The way of Taekwondo is a personal journey of development and a shared experience within the family of Taekwondo. Writing The Heart of Taekwondo has been very hard work, exhilarating and a truly rewarding experience. It gives me great pleasure to share my ideas, understanding and experiences with fellow practitioners. I will continue to train hard and strive to attain new goals with the 'determination' and 'spirit', shared by Taekwondo practitioners throughout the world. I hope you will continue to walk in the way of Taekwondo. Eat well, Move more, Rest well, Live longer. Enjoy this excellent quality of life.

Training continues.

Kind Regards

Grand Master

Mark Biddlecombe

Appendices

Appendix 7.1

Appendix 7.1

Various kinds of food arranged by their carbohydrate content, illustrating approximate levels of fuel that the body and mind can use once consumed and converted into glucose.

* Nutritional information is sourced from: The US Department of Agriculture.

Various kinds of food	Quantity	Carbohydrate Content (Grams)
Fruitcake	1 Cake	783
Carrot cake	1 Cake	775
Pecan pie	1 Pie	423
Cherry pie	1 Pie	363
Apple pie	1 Pie	360
Blueberry pie	1 Pie	330

Lemon meringue pie	1 Pie	317
Cheesecake	1 Cake	317
Gingerbread cake	1 Cake	291
Honey	1 Cup	279
Italian bread	1 Loaf	256
Ice-cream, vanilla	½ Gallon	254
French or Vienna bread	1 Loaf	230
White bread	1 Loaf	222
Custard pie	1 Pie	213
Mixed grain or Oatmeal bread	1 Loaf	212
Condensed milk	1 Cup	166
Danish pastry, plain (no nuts)	1 Ring	152
Rice, white, raw	1 Cup	149
Dates, chopped	1 Cup	131
Figs, dried	10 Figs	122
Raisins	1 Cup	115
Cranberry sauce	1 Cup	108
Peaches, dried	1 Cup	98
Orange juice, concentrate	6 Fl oz	81
Apricots, dried	1 Cup	80
Rhubarb	1 Cup	75

Raspberries and Strawberries	10 oz	74
Grapefruit juice	6 oz	72
Pecan pie	1 Piece	71
Cherry pie	1 Piece	61
Plums, canned in syrup	1 Cup	60
Chocolate milkshake, prunes	10 oz	60
Apple pie, peach pie	1 Piece	60
Sweet potatoes, canned	1 Cup	59
Apricots, canned	1 Cup	55
Lemon meringue pie	1 Piece	53
Pineapple, peaches, canned in syrup	1 Cup	52
Potatoes, baked with skin	1 Potato	51
Apple sauce	1 Cup	51
Rice, brown and white, cooked	1 Cup	50
Milkshake, vanilla	10 oz	50
Pears, canned in syrup	1 Cup	49
Fruit cocktail, canned in syrup	1 Cup	48

Carrot cake	1 Piece	48
Corn, canned	1 Cup	46
Orange soda	12 Fl oz	46
Cashew and dry roasted nuts	1 Cup	45
Yogurt	8 oz	43
Peas	1 Cup	42
Chicken pie	1 Piece	42
Red kidney beans, canned	1 Cup	42
Root beer and Cola, regular	12 Fl oz	42
Cheeseburger	4 oz sandwich	40
Macaroni and cheese	1 Cup	40
Pizza, cheese	1 Slice	39
Spaghetti, tomato sauce	1 Cup	39
Spaghetti meatballs, tomato sauce	1 Cup	39
Lentils, dry	1 Cup	38
Bagels, plain	1 Bagel	38
Hamburger	4 oz sandwich	38
Mashed potatoes	1 Cup	38
Custard pie	1 Piece	36
Watermelon	1 Piece	35
Bananas, sliced	1 Cup	35

Corn, yellow	1 Cup	34
Maple syrup	2 Tablespoons	32
Chocolate chip cookies	4 Biscuits	32
Ginger ale	12 Fl oz	32
Pears, canned	1 Cup	32
Chilli con carne, with beans	1 Cup	31
Parsnips	1 Cup	30
Cottage cheese	1 Cup	30
Popcorn, syrup coated	1 Cup	30
Chocolate pudding, canned	5 oz	30
Custard, cooked	1 Cup	29
Apple juice, canned	1 Cup	29
Quiche Lorraine	1 Slice	29
Evaporated milk, skimmed, canned	1 Cup	29
Peanut butter cookie	4 Cookies	28
Tapioca pudding, canned	5 oz	28
Boiled sweets	1 oz	28
Potato salad with mayonnaise	1 Cup	28
Almonds	1 Cup	28
English muffin, plain	1 Muffin	27

Peanuts, salted	1 Cup	27
Rice pudding	½ Cup	27
Banana	1 Banana	27
Croissants	1 Croissant	27
Pea soup	1 Cup	27
Orange juice	1 Cup	26
Jelly beans	1 oz	26
Noodles, chow mein	1 Cup	26
Doughnuts	1 Doughnut	26
Cornflakes cereal	1 oz	24
Shredded wheat cereal	1 oz	23
Apples, peeled	1 Cup	16
Beef and vegetable stew	1 Cup	15
Cream of chicken soup	1 Cup	15
Oranges	1 Orange	15
Mixed vegetables, canned	1 Cup	15
Jams and preserves	1 Tablespoon	14
Brown and chicken gravy	1 Cup	14
Whole-wheat bread, toasted	1 Slice	13
Brussels sprouts	1 Cup	13
Jellies	1 Tablespoon	13

Fried chicken breast	5 oz	13
Mixed grain bread	1 Slice	12
White bread, slice and toasted	1 Slice	12
Milk, skimmed	1 Cup	12
Vegetable soup, canned	1 Cup	12
Sugar, white, granulated	1 Tablespoon	12
Carrots	1 Cup	12
Kiwi fruit	1 Kiwi	11
Milk, whole	1 Cup	11
Scallops, breaded	6 Scallops	10
Grapes	10 Grapes	10
Crisps	10 Crisps	10
Broccoli	1 Cup	10
Tomatoes, canned	1 Cup	10
Spinach	1 Cup	10
Coffee	1 Cup	9
Pancakes	1 Pancake	9
Asparagus	1 Cup	9
Tangerines	1 Tangerine	9
Cream of mushroom soup	1 Cup	9
Haddock, breaded, fried	3 oz	7
Whipped cream	1 Cup	7

Eggplant	1 Cup	6
Cheese crackers	10 Crackers	6
Lemon	1 Lemon	5
Cauliflower	1 Cup	5
Cabbage, Savoy	1 Cup	5
Fish fingers	1 Stick	4
Lettuce	1 Head	4
Celery	1 Cup	4
Mayonnaise salad dressings	1 Tablespoon	4
Peppers, hot chilli	1 Pepper	4
Wine, table	3.5 Fl oz	3
Mushrooms	1 cup	3
Turkey roast	3 oz	3
Peanut butter	1 Tablespoon	3
French salad dressing	1 Tablespoon	2
1000 Island dressing	1 Tablespoon	2
Bacon	2 Slices	1
Eggs, fried, hard boiled, scrambled	1 Egg	1
Eggs raw	1 Egg	1
Pork luncheon meat, canned	2 Slices	1
Cheddar cheese, shredded	1 Cup	1
Tea	8 Fl oz	1
Instant coffee	6 Fl oz	1

Mozzarella cheese	1 oz	1
Sour cream	1 Tablespoon	1
Margarine	8 oz	1
Cucumber	6 Slices	1
Tartar sauce	1 Tablespoon	1
Sardines, canned	3 oz	0
Tuna fish, canned	3 oz	0
Parmesan cheese	1 Tablespoon	0
Beef roast, rib	3 oz	0
Salmon, smoked	3 oz	0
Salt	1 Tablespoon	0
Beef broth	1 Cup	0
Turkey loaf, breast meat	2 Slices	0
Cola, diet	12 Fl oz	0
Gin, Rum, Vodka, Whiskey, 90% proof	1.5 Fl oz	0
Olive oil	1 Cup	0
Lard	1 Cup	0
Butter	1 Tablespoon	0
Lamb chops	2.3 oz	0
Corned beef, canned	3 oz	0
Pork chop	2.5 oz	0
Vienna sausage	1 Sausage	0
Sunflower oil	1 Cup	0
Crabmeat	1 Cup	0
Olives, green, canned	4 Medium	0

Further Reading

Bearman, G., Graham, R., Riley, G. and Wardell, P. (eds) (2006) From Cells to Consciousness, Halstan, United Kingdom.
Bearman, G., Graham, R., Riley, G. and Wardell, P. (eds) (2006) Emotions and Mind, Halstan, United Kingdom.
Chun, R. (1976) Tae Kwon Do: The Korean Martial Art, Harper and Row, New York.
Chun, R. (1982) Advancing in Tae Kwon Do, Harper and Row, New York.
Held, D. (ed.) (2004) A Globalising World? Culture, Economics, Politics, Routledge, London.
Hibbard, J. (1981) Karate Breaking Techniques, Charles E. Tuttle, Japan.
Kalat, J. W. (1995) Biological Psychology: Fifth Edition, Brooks and Cole, USA.
Kang, L. and Song, N. (2008) The Explanation of Official Taekwondo Poomsae, Sang-a, Korea.
Kim, D. (1985) Complete One-step Fighting, Nanam, South Korea.
Kim, J. R. (1986) Taekwondo: Basic Techniques and Taegeuk Poomse, Seo Lim, Korea.
Kim, J. R. (1986) Taekwondo: Black Belt Level Poomse, Seo Lim, Korea.

Kukkiwon Taekwondo Academy (ed.) (2001) Taekwondo Instructor Course Textbook, Kukkiwon Taekwondo Academy, Korea.

Kukkiwon Taekwondo Academy (ed.) (2006) Taekwondo Instructor Course Textbook, Kukkiwon Taekwondo Academy, Korea.

Kukkiwon, World Taekwondo Headquarters (ed.) (2006) Taekwondo Textbook I, O-Sung, Korea.

Kukkiwon, World Taekwondo Headquarters (ed.) (2006) Taekwondo Textbook II, O-Sung, Korea.

Kukkiwon, World Taekwondo Headquarters (ed.) (2009) The 1st Seoul World Taekwondo Leaders Forum, Kukkiwon, Korea.

Kukkiwon, World Taekwondo Headquarters (ed.) (2009) The Textbook of Taekwondo Poomsae, O-Sung, Korea.

O'Brien, P. (1991) An Introduction to Tae Kwon Do, Macdonald Optima, London.

Park, Y. Hee, Park, Y. Hwan and Gerrard, J. (1989) Tae Kwon Do: The Ultimate Reference Guide to the World's Most Popular Martial Art, Facts On File, USA.

Park, Y. H. and Seabourne, T. (1997) Taekwondo Techniques and Tactics, Human Kinetics, USA.

Son, D. S. and Clark, R. J. (1983) Black Belt Korean Karate, Prentice-Hall, USA.

Woodward, K. (2003) Social Sciences: The Big Issues, Cromwell Press, Great Britain.

World Taekwondo Academy (ed.) (2009) The Taekwondo Park, Taekwondo Promotion Foundation, Korea.

World Taekwondo Federation (ed.) (2009) Bigger Than Ever, World Taekwondo Federation, Korea.